C. S. Lewis
and the Art of Writing

C. S. Lewis
and the Art of Writing

What the Essayist, Poet, Novelist, Literary Critic,
Apologist, Memoirist, Theologian Teaches Us
about the Life and Craft of Writing

COREY LATTA

CASCADE *Books* · Eugene, Oregon

C. S. LEWIS AND THE ART OF WRITING
What the Essayist, Poet, Novelist, Literary Critic, Apologist, Memoirist, Theologian
Teaches Us about the Life and Craft of Writing

Cascade Books
An Imprint of Wipf and Stock Publishers
199 W. 8th Ave., Suite 3
Eugene, OR 97401

www.wipfandstock.com

PAPERBACK ISBN: 978-1-4982-2534-2
HARDCOVER ISBN: 978-1-4982-2536-6
EBOOK ISBN: 978-1-4982-2535-9

Cataloguing-in-Publication data:

Names: Latta, Corey.

Title: C. S. Lewis and the art of writing : what the essayist, poet, novelist, literary
critic, apologist, memoirist, theologian teaches us about the life and craft of writing /
Corey Latta.

Description: Eugene, OR: Cascade Books, 2016 | Includes bibliographical references
and index.

Identifiers: ISBN 978-1-4982-2534-2 (paperback) | ISBN 978-1-4982-2536-6 (hardcover)
| ISBN 978-1-4982-2535-9 (ebook)

Subjects: LCSH: Lewis, C. S. (Clive Staples), 1898–1963—Criticism and interpretation |
Authorship | Fiction—technique | Writing | Creative writing

Classification: PR6023 L38 2016 (paperback) | PR6023 (ebook)

Manufactured in the U.S.A.   08/10/16

To Jennifer, whose patience is as beautiful a book as I've ever read.

This most of all: ask yourself in the most silent hour of your night: must I write? Dig into yourself for a deep answer. And if this answer rings out in assent, if you meet this solemn question with a strong, simple "I must," then build your life in accordance with this necessity; your whole life, even into its humblest and most indifferent hour, must become a sign and witness to this impulse.

RAINER MARIA RILKE, *LETTERS TO A YOUNG POET*

Obedience is an unpopular word nowadays, but the artist must be obedient to the work, whether it be a symphony, a painting, or a story for a small child. I believe that each work of art, whether it is a work of great genius or something very small, comes to the artist and says "Here I am. Enflesh me. Give birth to me."

MADELEINE L'ENGLE, *WALKING ON WATER*

Contents

Acknowledgements

C. S. Lewis and the Art of Writing only exists because of the help of my friends and colleagues. I owe the idea for this book to Dr. Jerry Root and to Dr. Jameela Lares, both exemplary models of scholarship, integrity, and faith. I'm particularly thankful for the wonderful services of the staff at the Wade Center and for Marjorie Lamp Mead. I'm also indebted to the inestimable editorial work of Marybeth Davis Baggett.

Ink to Cure All Human Ills

"Whenever you are fed up with life, start writing: ink is the great cure for all human ills, as I have found out long ago."

— Lewis, to Arthur Greeves

Readers know C. S. Lewis from his fantasy works, meeting the prolific author in the icy woods of Narnia, on the high vast plains of *The Great Divorce*, or on the paradisal seas of Perelandra. Just as many, if not more, know Lewis from his immensely influential apologetic works, each filled with eminently quotable passages. *Jesus must either be liar, lunatic, or Lord*; *Pain is God's megaphone to rouse a deaf world*; *Next to the Blessed Sacrament itself, your neighbor is the holiest object presented to your senses* provide memorable paths of familiarity to Lewis the theological thinker. Some know Lewis primarily from his professional scholarship as a prominent literature scholar, whose expertise in Medieval and Renaissance studies as well as literary theory produced contributions such as *The Discarded Image, An Experiment in Criticism*, and *English Literature in the Sixteenth Century*.

Despite Lewis's fame in several fields and his library of publications, very few, I'd wager, when they think of Lewis, consider him a writer's writer, a craftsman of English prose whose content proves inseverable from his lessons on *how* to write. *C. S. Lewis and the Art of Writing* means to meet Lewis on the field of composition and to acquaint Lewis's devotees with his identity as a master of the English language, a writer whose capacity for clarity, precision, and exemplary execution is matched only by the quality of his thinking.

C. S. Lewis and the Art of Writing

The reasons for this book are simple. First, to date, no one has taken on the task of writing about Lewis's philosophy, style, and craft of writing. It's worth knowing that Lewis never intended to be a famous theologian or bestselling fantasy novelist, as his preeminence in those areas may lead some to believe. He did, however, from a very early age want to be a writer— a poet, to be precise. Writerly desire, not unlike those early visitations of joyous yearning (*Sehnsucht*) he wrote about in *Surprised by Joy*, enduringly animated Lewis's early life. From his childhood world of *Boxen*, through his pre-Christian works of poetry *Spirits in Bondage* and *Dymer*, to the myriad of his post-conversion writings, fiction and non, Lewis demonstrated a tremendous affinity and capacity for clear, functional, and beautiful language. The dearth of work on Lewis's writing *as writing* is surprising. But dearth is opportunity. And Lewis's life and works are far from overdone as objects of study. If we with an interest in Lewis—either scholarly or amateur—are to deepen our knowledge of and affection for the great writer, then we must spend more time considering the life of his craft.

A second reason for this book is to pay homage to Lewis. No other prose writer, living or dead, has influenced me more in terms of style. Years of pouring over Lewis's work, both for pleasure and academic purposes, have indelibly impressed upon me the importance of effective language to convey—or omnibus, if you like—profound ideas. A watershed moment in my writing life came when my dissertation advisor, an accomplished Milton scholar, Anglophile, and avid Lewis lover, challenged my view of Lewis and called my craft to a higher plane. My dissertation analyzed C. S. Lewis, T. S. Eliot, and W. H. Auden's theology of time, as influenced, I argued, by French Philosopher Henri Bergson's theory of duration. In the fray of revisions, after submitting a relatively rough portion of the chapter on Lewis, my advisor said, "You're writing about one of the most clear and articulate writers of the twentieth century, so you had better write about him in a worthy manner."

She was right. I had better. And I did. When I began to pay close attention to the *way* Lewis wrote, I appreciated *what* he wrote about all the more. His writing not only transmits his ideas, it vivifies them. The danger of self-protection in *The Four Loves* finds its force in the alliterative cadence of Lewis's syntax, when he warns that the invulnerable heart "will become unbreakable, impenetrable, irredeemable." It's Lewis mastery of the asylumed image that makes an otherwise obvious idea so forcible: "A man can no more diminish God's glory by refusing to worship Him than a lunatic can put out the sun by scribbling the word 'darkness' on the walls of his cell." Again, "Aim at heaven and you will get Earth 'thrown in': aim at Earth and you will get neither," which Lewis writes in *Mere Christianity*, is a profound truth, one on which I've tried to center my life. But the power of this proposition, what actually deploys this Matthean idea (Matt 6:33), is its functional diction, its symmetrical rhythm, its play on verb tense, its simple clarity.

We can't properly study Lewis's ideas without stopping to consider how exquisitely he states them. Indeed, there is no divorce, great or otherwise, between the ideological and textual in Lewis's prose worlds. Mindful travelers must be aware of both truth and turn of phrase, of both the verbal incarnation of a thought and its inflection. Indeed, when we venture into Lewis's writing, we enter into a vista of beauty and meaning. All is clear. We must be keener observers and careful imitators. For writers, whose struggle to embody ideas through language will ever endure, Lewis proves an example of complex thinking through lucid prose. May that alone be reason enough for those who claim the call of writer to study his craft.

A final reason for this book comes from one of Lewis's letters, written to a young American Narnia enthusiast with aspiring interests in writing named Joan Lancaster. Found in *Letters to Children*, Lewis's letter to Joan emphasizes "what really matters" in crafting prose. The letter reads:

> The Kilns,
> Headington Quarry,
> Oxford
> 26 June 1956

> Dear Joan –

> Thanks for your letter of the 3rd. You describe your Wonderful Night v. well. That is, you describe the place and the people and the night and the feeling of it all, very well—but not the *thing* itself—the setting but not the jewel. And no wonder! Wordsworth often does just the same. His *Prelude* (you're bound to read it about 10 years hence. Don't try it now, or you'll only spoil it for later reading) is full of moments in which everything except the *thing* itself is described. If you become a writer you'll be trying to describe the *thing* all your life: and lucky if, out of dozens of books, one or two sentences, just for a moment, come near to getting it across.

> About *amn't I, aren't I* and *am I not*, of course there are no right or wrong answers about language in the sense in which there

are right and wrong answers in Arithmetic. "Good English" is whatever educated people talk; so that what is good in one place or time would not be so in another. *Amn't I* was good 50 years ago in the North of Ireland where I was brought up, but bad in Southern England. *Aren't I* would have been hideously bad in Ireland but very good in England. And of course I just don't know which (if either) is good in modern Florida. Don't take any notice of teachers and textbooks in such matters. Nor of logic. It is good to say "more than one passenger was hurt," although *more than one* equals at least two and therefore logically the verb ought to be plural *were* not singular *was*!

What really matters is:—

1. Always try to use the language so as to make quite clear what you mean and make sure your sentence couldn't mean anything else.

2. Always prefer the plain direct word to the long, vague one. Don't *implement* promises, but *keep* them.

3. Never use abstract nouns when concrete ones will do. If you mean "More people died' don't say "Mortality rose."

4. In writing. Don't use adjectives which merely tell us how you want us to *feel* about the thing you are describing. I mean, instead of telling us a thing was "terrible," describe it so that we'll be terrified. Don't say it was "delightful"; make *us* say "delightful" when we've read the description. You see, all those words (horrifying, wonderful, hideous, exquisite) are only like saying to your readers, "Please will you do my job for me."

5. Don't use words too big for the subject. Don't say "infinitely" when you mean "very"; otherwise you'll have no word left when you want to talk about something *really* infinite.

Thanks for the photos. You and Aslan both look v. well. I hope you'll like your new home.

With love
yours
C. S. Lewis

While Lewis offers practical and theoretical guidance on writing several times in several works, this letter is one of his most explicit, itemized, and practical pieces of advice on writing. Here, Lewis delineates his essential advice for the prose writer. The five prescriptions Lewis puts forth—1) make quite clear what you mean, 2) prefer the plain, 3) never use abstract

if writing meaning gives meaning to life

nouns when concrete ones will do, 4) instead of telling us a thing, describe it, and 5) don't use words too big for the subject—prove helpful to any writer in any genre, and perhaps more importantly, reveal writerly principles vital for understanding Lewis's acclaimed ability to communicate profound thought through clear language with seemingly universal appeal.

And Lewis lived his advice. His commitment to clarity, plainness, concrete nouns, descriptive language, and proportionate diction create an accessibility that enables readers from all ages and various intellectual life stations to enjoy works like *Mere Christianity*, *The Screwtape Letters*, and *The Chronicles of Narnia*. Those same guiding principles may be found in Lewis's more academic books as well: *Studies in Words*, *The Problem of Pain*, and *Four Loves* to name just a few for now. In his letter to Joan Lancaster, Lewis has effectively identified those compositional rules that elevate the elementary and make elementary the elevated.

Another point of introduction is in order. In a letter addressed to life-long friend Arthur Greeves, seventeen-year-old C. S. Lewis admonished Greeves with the following advice, a claim I hold to be the ultimate purpose for *C. S. Lewis and the Art of Writing*: "Whenever you are fed up with life, start writing: ink is the great cure for all human ills, as I have found out long ago." Writers are a rare artistic breed, creatures who burden under the illusion that the boundaries of fear and ill fate, melancholy and mediocrity, hopelessness and heartbreak bend and break by the power of pen and paper. The test of whether someone is a *real* writer is not what or where he has published; neither is it if he writes professionally for a living. Rather the mark of a real writer is whether his writing gives meaning to life. Lewis embodied this. His love for and dedication to the craft of writing were met daily by the extraordinary personal meaning it gave him. His letters, from which I will continually draw, underscore Lewis's mastery over, devotion to, and love for words. There is hardly an area of Lewis's life untouched by writing. Every relationship. Every loss. Every fear. Every ambition. Every hope. Every disappointment. His life-changing conversion to Christ. His brilliance. Quite literally, writing composes the meaning of Lewis's life experiences.

To say that Lewis believed writing had this kind of meaning-making power is a gross understatement. From his childhood, when books beautified his view of the world, through his unbelieving era prior to his dejectedly admitting that "God was God" and turning to the Christian faith, and throughout his post-conversion years, which saw the vast majority of his literary output, Lewis's life testifies to writing's ability to transform both head and heart. Lewis saw writing as far more than a matter of precise craft and a means of personal comfort. For Lewis, writing was the prism through which the Divine light that "lighteneth every man" shines, as he reminds readers in his essay, "Is Theology Poetry?" Lewis shows us that writing makes meaning, that all meaning belongs to God, and that God, the eternal Word, reveals Himself through writing.

Lewis fleshes out the revelatory power of writing in *Till We Have Faces*, perhaps Lewis's most superb work of literary fiction. In the novel, Orual, the chief character, captures her creator's high view of writing in a particularly revealing passage about the art and difficulty of exact language:

> Lightly men talk of saying what they mean. Often when he was teaching me to write in Greek the Fox would say, "Child, to say the very thing you really mean, the whole of it, nothing more or less or other than what you really mean; that's the whole art and joy of words."
>
> A glib saying. When the time comes to you at which you will be forced at last to utter the speech which has lain at the center of your soul for years which you have, all that time, idiot-like, been saying over and over, you'll not talk about the joy of words. I saw well why the gods do not speak to us openly, nor let us answer. Till that word can be dug out of us, why should they hear the babble that we think we mean? How can they meet us face to face till we have faces?

Till We Have Faces is interested in the revealing role of language, in how the *logos*, both written and spoken, moves. Here, Orual recalls Fox's advice on an exact way of writing, claiming that the ability to say "nothing more or less or other than what you really mean" is the "art and joy"—an interesting pairing for Lewis—of writing.

However, for Orual as for Lewis, something deeper than the joy of discourse lies beneath the precise use of language. Orual thinks beyond Fox's glib maxim, confessing her own reflections about the essence of human expression. Through language the divine meets us at the center of our being, where our deepest words lie. To dig down beyond the babbled rubble of language, to till beyond the art and joy of words, and ultimately, to say what has been laid at the center of our souls is writing's proper function. Lewis would have us learn that in writing, in revealing what lies in the center of ourselves, we know something of the divine, and therefore, something of ourselves. In exploring the ways Lewis wrote, in he how approached the craft, *C. S. Lewis and the Art of Writing* will attempt to delve into the center of who Lewis was as a writer in hopes of better knowing those deeply-dug words he so eloquently uttered.

One last introductory word about what this book is and what it is not: *C. S. Lewis and the Art of Writing* is about Lewis's writing life. And because every life has a beginning, a middle full of important thoughts and moments, and an end, this book will be somewhat biographical. Each chapter is short and meant to frame moments from Lewis's life in—and his advice on—writing. My approach is eclectic. The chapters are anecdotal and meant to leave the writer with one or two pressing themes. I have chosen chapter topics by how insightful I think they are into Lewis's creative development, by how they demonstrate his approach to the craft of writing, and by how they advise writers. I have found Lewis's collected letters the most invaluable resource for studying Lewis's writing life, and any instance of dependence on them brings the writer's life into the conversation of craft. The chapters on the influence reading had on Lewis's craft and those on Lewis's experiences with the process and profession of writing are unapologetically biographical. Pertinent bits from Lewis's childhood, important moments and musings in his lifelong practice of writing, and those important creative bursts nearing the end of his life are very much this book's scope.

In addition to being biographical, *C. S. Lewis and the Art of Writing* is a work of tell and show. The last five chapters are devoted to Lewis's letter to young Joan Lancaster, to whom he offers imitable advice on how to be a better writer. In these last chapters, I will explain, or "tell," each piece of advice Lewis offered—"make quite clear what you mean," for example—and then proceed to demonstrate, or "show," how Lewis's writing exemplifies the point. In this pattern of telling and showing, I hope to be practical, to give other writers something helpful to take hold of as they practice their craft.

Since the purpose of *C. S. Lewis and the Art of Writing* is to be practical, readers will find "for the writer" notes at the end of each chapter. These are meant only to be helpful creative spurs: informative, provocative, and simple considerations for anyone serious about the craft of writing. As Lewis once encouragingly wrote to Arthur Greeves, "practice, practice, practice." Perhaps *C. S. Lewis and the Art of Writing* will serve well as a resource for writers whose first duty is to practice.

Above all, and this proves tricky for any writer, I want readers to hear Lewis's words over my own. I want his voice to increase and mine to decrease. This, finally, leads to what this book is not. In *Mere Christianity*, Lewis writes that "even in literature and art, no man who bothers about originality will ever be original: whereas if you simply try to tell the truth (without caring twopence how often it has been told before) you will, nine times out of ten, become original without ever having noticed it."

In that vein, *C. S. Lewis and the Art of Writing* does not aim at being clever or artificially original. I have no intention of offering a tantalizing new reading of Lewis's work. I want fans of Lewis from all walks of life and with all sorts of interests to know Lewis for what he gave much of his life to being, a writer. So may this book tell the truth. May it, I dare say, be unoriginal.

Of Endless Books

Have you noticed how God so often sends us books
at just the right time?

— LETTER TO DOM BEDE GRIFFITHS

Those of us who have been true readers all our life seldom fully realize the
enormous extension of our being which we owe to authors.

— AN EXPERIMENT IN CRITICISM

Talking of books—you might ask, when do I talk of anything else . . .

— LETTER TO ARTHUR GREEVES

We cannot divorce Lewis the writer from Lewis the reader. Only a short time spent in his letters or the literarily allusive pages of his prose proves how the writer grew into solid reality from the reader. To say it another way, aim at Lewis the reader and you get the writer thrown in. The chapters in "Of Endless Books" aim at Lewis the reader. In this section, we'll see the ways Lewis's relationship with books created a writer.

I

How Reading Made a Writer

Lewis, once described as the "best-read man of his generation" and "one who read everything and remembered everything he read," wrote from the overflow of a life saturated in reading.[1] From the beginning of Lewis's creative life there existed a literary fountainhead from which ran a fast current of story, imaginative ideas, and other worlds and words that would flow through the entirety of his life. To appreciate Lewis as a writer—and preeminently as a writer whose philosophy and practice of writing stands as example to other writers—we do well to begin where his craft began, in a habitual life of reading.

Lewis, to whom the craft of writing came naturally and from whom it flowed powerfully, read himself into the writing life. When we meet the man behind his many books, we find a writer whose indelible induction into the creative life came early. It is telling that in his spiritual autobiography *Surprised by Joy* Lewis introduces the reader to his parents through what they read. About his mother Lewis tells us,

> she was a voracious reader of good novels, and I think the Merediths and Tolstoys which I have inherited were bought for her.[2]

And of his father,

---

1. James Como attributes this line to William Empson in *Remembering C. S. Lewis*, 35.

2. Lewis, *Surprised by Joy*, 4.

"he was fond of poetry . . . ; I think *Othello* was his favorite Shakespearean play" and "he greatly enjoyed nearly all humorous authors, from Dickens to W. W. Jacobs."[3]

Providence, it seems, placed Lewis in a home ideally nurturing for a future writer. Lewis inherited his parents' love for literature, but not their exact tastes. The mythic and romantic literary affinities Lewis would hold as an adolescent and adult—stories that rang with the "horns of elfland" and the poetry of Keats and Shelley—were not passed along by his parents. But an absence of faerie and romantic verse did little to deprive Lewis of a richly formative literary childhood. The influence of writers and words suffused his young years. In describing his lettered childhood, Lewis has quite a lot to say about the presence and importance of books:

> I am a product of long corridors, empty sunlit rooms, upstairs indoor silences, attics explored in solitude, distant noises of gurgling cisterns and pipes, and the noise of wind under the tiles. Also, of endless books. My father bought all the books he read and never got rid of any of them. There were books in the study, books in the drawing room, books, books in the cloakroom, books (two deep) in the great bookcase on the landing, books in a bedroom, books piled as high as my shoulder in the cistern attic, books of all kinds reflecting every transient stage of my parents' interest, books readable and unreadable, books suitable for a child and books most emphatically not. Nothing was forbidden me. In the seemingly endless rainy afternoons I took volume after volume from the shelves. I had always the same certainty of finding a book that was new to me as a man who walks into a field has of finding a new blade of grass . . . .[4]

Lewis's early life bears witness that a good writer is first a good reader. How telling that the author whose body of writing would so widely range from the philosophical non-fiction to the poetic to the fantastical children's story should spend his earliest years in a readerly panopticon. All manner of imaginative world and literary genre were available to him. Decades later, in *An Experiment in Criticism* published near the end of his life, Lewis would write of reading's power to provide new ways to see the world, saying simply that "we demand windows."[5] As Lewis learned early, escape lies

---

3. Ibid., 4–5.

4. Ibid., 10.

5. Lewis, *An Experiment in Criticism*, 138.

within good reading. Down the halls and stacked two deep on the shelves were windows that opened to young Jack—a self-appointed nickname from early childhood that Lewis kept through adulthood—cosmoses of written creation.

Lewis spent hours in a seemingly omnipresent solitude, which he writes, was always at his command.[6] The quiet attic made an apt workshop for a burgeoning brilliant mind. There in the silence of his childhood home, with its corridors of countless volumes, quaint hours reading and writing foreshadowed a life in letters. The more connections between his reading life and his craft—how, for example, his reading certain books directly influenced certain writings—will become more evident, but we should first go a bit further up and further into reading's systemic effect on Lewis's creative development.

"Alone in a big house full of books. I suppose that fixed a literary bent. I drew a lot, but soon began to write more."[7] For Lewis, reading and writing flourished simultaneously. He began to call the quiet attic his "study," a space lined with drawings and magazine cutouts, furnished with "Jack's desk," and stocked with "pen and inkpot and writing books and paintbox."[8] There young Jack began his writing life. In recounting the beginning of his writing life, Lewis quotes a line from Edmund Spenser, "What more felicity can fall to creature, than to enjoy delight with liberty."[9] Finding meaning in a passage he read then quoting that passage to describe his initiation into writing: how like Lewis! The Spenser quote is apt. Writing for Jack was pure cheer. His deft use of quotes, a move Lewis constantly makes throughout his non-fiction works, shows a writer on whom nothing read was lost.

For the writer

Lewis's literary history began with a childhood among books. His story tells a universal truth: writers are born from reading. The writer learns creativity by reading creative works. The writer's imagination widens through exposure to imaginative stories. The writer develops an intuitive feel for language by spending time with the written word. To start writing, start reading.

6. Lewis, *Surprised by Joy*, 12.
7. Quoted in Jacobs, *The Narnian*, xviii–xix.
8. See also Hooper in his introduction to *Boxen*, 8.
9. Spenser, "The Fate of the Butterflie," quoted in *Surprised by Joy*, 13.

When did you first start reading? What was the literary culture in your home like as a child? How did your childhood reading life affect your entry into writing?

Do try: In at least 500 words, write about your first memorable experience with books. Talk about the role early reading played in your imaginative life. Be personal, insightful, and creative.

2

The Glories of Childhood

During the dawn of his reading and writing life, Lewis's discriminating judgment of books began to take shape. We've seen that young Lewis had a taste for faerie and romance, how he longed to hear the "horns of elfland." His literary palate would be refined over the years, though never so much to diminish his appetite for faerie stories and tales of romance. It seems that Lewis read everything he could, and most everything he read left an impression. But those books that did not fan the flames of elfland and romance stood the best chances of losing his affection:

> of the books that I read at this time very few have quite faded from memory, but not all have retained my love. Conan Doyle's *Sir Nigel* . . . I have never felt inclined to reread.[1]

> Still less would I now read Mark Twain's *A Connecticut Yankee in King Arthur's Court* . . .[2]

Doyle's *Sir Nigel* is a good example of how early reading helped etch themes into Lewis's writing.[3] Even in Doyle he found a fondness for "knights in armour," and in Twain, elements of Arthurian romance. These

1. Lewis, *Surprised by Joy,* 14.

2. Ibid. *A Connecticut Yankee in King Arthur's Court,* published in 1889, is about an engineer from Connecticut transported back to the time of King Arthur.

3. *Sir Nigel* is a historical novel set during the *Hundred Year's War* about the heroic expedition of a knight named Nigel Loring in the service of King Edward III. *Nigel* was published in serial form in *The Strand Magazine* between December 1905 and December 1906.

tropes would remain lodged in Lewis's creative consciousness, appearing in Narnia's knightly motifs—for example, "Rise up, Sir Peter Wolf's-Bane" in *Prince Caspian*—and the Ransom Trilogy's Arthurian figures, such as "Master Merlin, wisest of the Britons, possessor of the secrets" in *That Hideous Strength*.[4]

More than to Doyle and Twain, Lewis was drawn to Edith Nesbit. When considering Lewis's development as a writer, it is important to remember, as goes the imagination, so goes the writing. One could make the case that much of the fiction Lewis would go on to write derived from what he read in the first two decades of his life. His childhood reading formed his imagination, which in turn formed the kinds of stories he wanted to write. In fiction, Lewis rarely wrote about anything that he wasn't first awakened to by reading.

In a letter from 1953, long after his writing career was well established, Lewis, in the context of discussing rereading old books, testifies to the importance of those childhood reading years:

> About re-reading books: I find like you that those read in my earlier 'teens often have no appeal, but this is not nearly so often true of those read in earlier childhood. . . . [I]t seems that the glories of childhood and the glories of adolescence are separated by a howling desert during which one was simply a greedy, cruel, spiteful little animal and imagination, in all but the lowest form, was asleep.[5]

If Lewis's imagination was anything, it was awake. It's not too much to say Lewis may well be one of the most literate men to have ever lived, not only because he read so many books—though I cannot think of another writer who read more widely or deeply—but because the books he read remained so close to him for so long. As a childhood writer, Lewis's imagination was under the sway of books that would bend his creative thinking for years to come.

Nesbit's writing certainly held sway, foreshadowing themes in Lewis's later fantasies. Her novel features four children whose mother has been ill in Malta. The children's father is away reporting the Russo-Japanese war. We can see the parallels between Nesbit's four adolescent characters and Narnia's Pevensies, they, too, separated from their parents. Lewis first found

---

4. Lewis, *The Lion, the Witch and the Wardrobe*, 133; Lewis, *That Hideous Strength*, 266.

5. Hooper, *Collected Letters* 3:396.

and fell for the ancient idea of the "dark backward and abysm of time" in Nesbit's *The Story of the Amulet*.[6] Once we enter through the wardrobe's doors and catch sight of castle Cair Paravel in *The Lion, the Witch and the Wardrobe* or wander through Glome's gates into the archaic pagan world of *Till We Have Faces*, we begin to see how Lewis the reader begot Lewis the writer.

For the writer

The imagination has memory. Themes met early in life show up in books later in life. Often enough, the writer need look no further than childhood to find them. Good writers spend the rest of their lives looking back to the images and ideas that first animated their thinking and awakened their imaginations.

What ideas captivated your imagination when you were a child? What was it about them that grabbed your attention? Did those ideas stay with you as you grew up? Which ideas still give you imaginative life?

Do try: Think of one idea or image from your childhood that awakened your imagination. Spend at least thirty minutes free writing about what it meant—and still means—to you.

---

6. Published in 1906, *The Story of the Amulet*, a children's book about an amulet with the power to enable time travel, was the final book in a trilogy, preceded by *Five Children and It* and *The Phoenix and the Carpet*.

3

Entirely in the Imagination

Some books imprinted upon Lewis with greater degree of permanence than did others. Lewis wrote in *Surprised by Joy*, "It will be clear that at this time—at the age of six, seven, and eight—I was living almost entirely in my imagination."[1]

Then came the Beatrix Potter books, and as he declared, "here at last beauty."[2] Potter's *Squirrel Nutkin* worked on Jack in two ways.[3] First, it helped awaken an intense yearning for another world, a joyous and uncanny "Idea of Autumn," Lewis writes. Though this incipient desire for joy—a longing, says Lewis, worth more than all the pleasures of the world and the central story of his life—felt autumnal, it proved to be a creative spring.

Potter's writing was most welcome to a child already living in his imagination. In Lewis's earliest creative years, there remained a disconnect between his written worlds and his imagination. His early childhood stories of "Animal Land" were quite prosaic, tales without poetry or romance or wonder. Lewis encountered Potter at a time when his first experiences of joy were creating in the writer a lifelong desire for something beyond, something wholly *other*.

This sense of otherness, a yearning Lewis labeled *Sehnsucht*, came through a few diverse moments, but it was his brother Warnie who gave

---

1. Lewis, *Surprised by Joy*, 15.

2. Ibid.

3. *The Tale of Squirrel Nutkin* (1903) is a children's book about a bold squirrel's escape from an owl.

Lewis his first taste of beauty. Warnie once brought into the nursery a small biscuit tin filled with moss, twigs, and flowers crafting a "toy garden" that gave Lewis an almost embryonic sense of Paradise. Lewis had another experience of *Sehnsucht*, or joy, when he caught a whiff of a blooming currant bush on a summer day. To describe this moment, "the memory of a memory" that felt centuries old, transporting him back to his brother's toy garden, Lewis turned to Milton. Lewis said in *Surprised by Joy*,

> It is difficult to find words strong enough for the sensation which came over me; Milton's "enormous bliss" of Eden (giving the full, ancient meaning to "enormous") comes somewhere near it.[4]

Ultimately, that Lewis awoke to "enormous bliss" matters for his conversion to Christianity. But more immediate to Lewis's early life, the writings of Beatrix Potter corroborated with Warnie's toy garden and the currant bush to create spiritual longing for otherness. In Potter's *Squirrel Nutkin*, Lewis experienced the shock of another dimension, something "quite different from ordinary life and even from ordinary pleasure" through a distinct literary form.[5] Potter's autumnal otherness came specifically through story at a time when Lewis was training to be a novelist.

Lewis is here emphatic about what kind of literature he wanted to write: "note well, a novelist; not a poet."[6] And this is the second way Potter's story worked on Lewis. It paired joy with story. George Sayer has said that Lewis spent the rest of his life searching for more of the joy he found in his brother's toy garden and in Potter.[7] We see that search in the pages of *The Great Divorce*, with its offers of everlasting joy, in *The Lion, the Witch and the Wardrobe* with the Pevensie's warmed hearts at first hearing Aslan's name, and in the allure of *Perelandra's* Deep Heaven. Not only did Lewis devote his spiritual life to knowing this joy more deeply; he also spent his creative life marrying it to fiction.

Poetry also had a vital place in Lewis's early experiences of *Sehnsucht*, and therefore, in his formation as a writer. After the shock of unsatisfied desire administered from reading *Squirrel Nutkin*, Lewis encountered the the vast northernness of Henry Wadsworth Longfellow's translation of Swedish writer Esaias Tegner's "Drapa":

4. Ibid., 16.
5. Ibid., 17.
6. Ibid., 15.
7. Sayer, *Jack*, 52.

I heard a voice that cried,
Balder the beautiful
Is dead, is dead[8]

This lifted Lewis "into huge regions of northern sky."[9] While he had never heard of Balder nor had any reason to care about his death, reading about him left Lewis reeling with a longing for a world he had never known. A couple of years would pass before poetry truly seized Lewis's heart, but Tegner's poem was the first spasm of meaning.

Lewis's love for poetry persisted, even when feelings of joy from reading it did not. By the time Lewis read Matthew Arnold's tragic narrative poem "Sohrab and Rustum," he had slipped into a joyless period of life, a season absent "authentic joy."[10] Lewis notes that while the poem brought only pleasure, not joy, it proved "the most important thing that happened" at a boarding school called Campbell that Lewis attended for a short time.

"Sohrab and Rustum" brought a sense of "passionate, silent gazing at things a long way off."[11] This was an important text for Lewis. It taught him "how literature actually works."[12] Lewis goes into some detail on the importance of Arnold's work to him and the inability of literary criticism to truly get at the meaning of a text: "Parrot critics say that 'Sohrab' is a poem for classicists, to be enjoyed only by those who recognize Homeric echoes . . . but I . . . knew nothing of Homer."[13] For Lewis, it worked the other way around.

When he finally came to Homer, Lewis liked it all the more because he had first read "Sohrab." It doesn't matter how you get into European poetry, as long as you do get in. If you "only keep your ears open and your mouth shut and everything will lead you to everything else in the end . . . ."[14] Literature opens windows to itself. Text reminds of text. One work

8. Lewis, *Surprised by Joy*, 17. Esaias Tegner was a nineteenth-century Swedish writer, whose *Frithiof's Saga* was published in 1825. Balder is the son of Odin in Norse Mythology.

9. Ibid.

10. Ibid., 72. Poet Matthew Arnold's "Sohrab and Rustum: An Episode" is a long narrative poem published in 1853.

11. Ibid., 53.

12. Ibid.

13. Ibid.

14. Ibid.

recalls another, leads to another, enlightens another—"Each part emitting its radiance to each other part."[15]

For the writer

Reading inspires. Lewis met the most powerful desire of his life, *Sehnsucht*, in books. Had Lewis never experienced this desirous yearning as a child it's likely that he wouldn't have gone on to write some of the books he did as an adult. *Sehnsucht* moved through texts Lewis read. So it goes with writers and powerful truths. Ideas and feelings spawned by literature stir the writer's heart and move as a Muse in her imagination. Good writers see the beauty in a story and allow themselves to be swayed by it.

What books have been transcendent in your life? How have they worked in your life creatively and spiritually? If you had to say there was a theme in your life—as *Sehnsucht* was in Lewis's—what would it be?

Do try: In 750–1,000 words, write about a truth, idea, or belief that has profoundly shaped your life. Be specific in discussing how this truth has influenced you. Be descriptive. Tell a story.

---

15. From Dante's *Inferno* VII, line 75, which Lewis quotes in *Surprised by Joy*, 53.

4

Engulfed

Naturally, one's primary school plays an important part in literacy. While Lewis spared no criticism of his years bouncing around in English Boarding Schools, some experiences helped to redeem the time. While at Wynyard, or "Concentration Camp" as Lewis calls it, he encountered the works of Rider Haggard and H. G. Wells. Christian novelist Graham Greene said about Haggard,

> Enchantment is just what this writer exercised; he fixed pictures in our minds that thirty years have been unable to wear away.[1]

For a young reader awakening to the fantastic as Lewis was, Haggard's imaginative force left an impression. Lewis found solace and escape in Haggard's stories, returning to them faithfully over the years.

Wells's interplanetary "scientification" introduced a new affection. Unlike the joy of Lewis's earlier reading life, this new planetary pull "was something coarser and stronger," creating what he describes as a ravenous lust, a peculiar psychological effect.[2] Wells influenced Lewis's own planetary romance, and his delving into that genre was as much an exorcism as a gratification of his desire for sci-fi.

At twelve years old, Lewis developed an intense love for Faerie. On a long Christmas holiday, a time when Lewis could enter "with complete satisfaction into a deeper solitude" than he had ever known, a time when

---

1. Greene, "Rider Haggard's Secret," 209.
2. Lewis, *Surprised by Joy*, 36.

he could "read, write, and draw" to his heart's content, he "fell deeply under the spell of Dwarfs."[3] The spell would last a lifetime. The deposit fairy stories made to Lewis's imagination would have tremendous returns. *The Chronicles of Narnia* are Lewis's primary contribution to Faerie, but essays like "Sometimes Fairy Stories May Say Best What's to be Said," a defense of Faerie's unique ability to convey its themes, iterate the importance to Lewis of embracing fairy as a distinct kind of literature. His newfound fondness for fairy stories took Lewis to the edges of the supernatural. The otherness sparked by Potter and Tegner began to creep back in again. Until this time, Lewis had been in an imaginative lull.

The lull truly broke when Lewis happened upon *Siegfried and the Twilight of the Gods*, a volume illustrated by Arthur Rackham that gave him the same Northern "vision of huge, clear spaces" he met in Balder.[4]

> Pure "Northernness" engulfed me . . . and almost at the same moment I knew that I had met this before, long, long ago in Tegner's *Drapa*, that *Siegfried* (whatever it might be) belonged to the same world as Balder and the sunward-sailing cranes.[5]

With *Siegfried*, we have the first of many instances when something Lewis read directly caused something he wrote. Mused by Wagner's *The Ring of the Nibelung*, the synopses of which he found in a magazine called *The Soundbox*, Lewis "could contain himself no longer" and so "began a poem, a heroic poem on the Wagnerian version of the Nibelung story."[6]

In an exploration into Lewis's development as a writer, this creative outburst is significant in two ways. First, in his attempt at Siegfried's "The Nibelung" poem, Lewis had become a poet. Throughout the rest of his life, Lewis would return to poetry as an important channel through which would rush voices of inspiration. Lewis wrote poetry because he first read poetry. This correlation between input and output models the making of a writer. And it's here, in this matter of making, that we see a second point of significance.

About his Nibelung poem, Lewis wrote,

3. Ibid., 54.

4. Ibid., 53, 73.

5. Ibid., 73.

6. Ibid., 74.

the reader will not be surprised to hear that the poem was never finished. But it was not a waste of time, and I can still see just what it did for me and where it began to do it.[7]

Lewis was, on occasion, a non-finisher. His unfinished Nibelung poem reveals a normal part of Lewis's writing process: the moment when you as a writer know to say to your labor, "there is nothing more I can do with you." Or, perhaps, the moment when the book looks at you to say, "there is nothing more I can do with you." Throughout Lewis's writing life, we see moments of both.

For the writer

Writers work from inspiration, siphoning those ideas that give them creative life. Periods of productivity can come in and after time spent engulfed in a book that has captured the writer's heart. The wise writer who finds himself lost in a book and under its spell will spend his creative energy exercising that enchantment. Good writers know that books are an endless source of inspiration. They return to them repeatedly in search of enchantment.

What is the last inspiring idea you've come across in a book? What about it was inspiring? How has—or how can—inspiration worked out practically in your creative life? Have you written about it?

Do try: Write about the role of inspiration in writing. Try to stay focused on inspiration from reading. Explain how you experience inspiration, how you move from reading to being enchanted, to internalizing, to actually writing. Spend at least thirty minutes putting your thoughts on the page.

7. Ibid.

26

5

I Myself Have Been Reading

Beyond learning forms of fiction, feeling experiences of escape, and longing for vast open northern skies from Nesbit, Potter, Tegner, and Wagner's *Ring of Nibelung*, reading quickly became far more personally important to Lewis. It's unsurprising that to see a man as a writer, as we are doing, we ought also to see the writer as a man. Of life informing writing, and writing, life, Lewis is a superb example. Books found their way into his every, especially his closest, relationship. His devotion to disciplined reading defined his daily life rhythm. Lewis's relationship with reading offers invaluable insights into his creative formation. We need only look at Lewis's letters to see the ways his reading life started to meld into, and in some ways become, his personal life.

Within his letters lies the most transparent account of the man, thinker, and writer. Personally, Lewis's reading life remained a bond between him and those closest to him; sometimes it seems the strongest bond. Hardly a letter exists that doesn't include Lewis's reporting on or recommending a book he had read or was reading. His relationship with his father Albert bears this out. The two continually exchanged thoughts on their reading lives, until Lewis's father died in 1929.

Lewis filled almost twenty-five years of writing letters to his father with comments that reveal the role reading played in their relationship:

> I am at present engaged in reading Newman's poems: do you know them at all?[1]

1. Hooper, *Collected Letters* 1.65. Lewis referred to Newman's *Verses on Various*

I myself have been reading this week a book by a man named Love Peacock . . . .[2]

I am still busy with my "heavy winged Pegasus" as you call Spenser, and still find him delightful. . . . I have also been reading in library copies, Schopenhauer's "Will and Idea," and Swinburne's "Erectheus" . . . .[3]

Our own friend "Pilgrim's Progress." It is one of those books that are usually read too early to appreciate, and perhaps don't come back to. I am very glad however to have discovered it.[4]

Lewis had little clue that some of the books he read before his Christian conversion would show themselves in his post-conversion writing. Though Lewis thought Bunyan's *Pilgrim's Progress* an obvious, even childish, allegory, he valued it as an unsurpassable romance and superb work of English. How time and heart can change. Not only is the title of the first work Lewis would write after becoming a Christian *Pilgrim's Regress*, a play on Bunyan's *Progress*, but the plot and level of allegory in *Regress* are remarkably imitative. In terms of influential literature, Bunyan was one of several providential preconversion reads that shaped Lewis's artistic sensibilities.

Sharing his thoughts on Schopenhauer, Bunyan, or whatever book he was currently reading was an important part of Lewis's correspondence with his father. These conversations about literature served a relational need for the two, providing a means of fellowship at times when little else could. On a deeply personal level, Lewis's relationship with his father was often strained—particularly after the death of his mother when Lewis was not yet ten—and reading gave them a common bond. Once off to boarding school, his reading life always afforded something for Lewis to write home about. In a letter written from Malvern, the infamously hated boarding school Lewis attended between 1913 and 1914, Lewis wrote to tell his father of the writing assignments his Classics teacher, a man whom Lewis admired and fondly called "Smugy," had set for the class.

The choices were a poem in the style of Horace about "asking a friend to stay with you at the most beautiful spot you know," a picture of a specific

---

Occasions.

2. Ibid., 150.

3. Ibid., 151.

4. Ibid., 247.

scene from Sophocles, or an original ghost story."[5] Lewis added, "as you have probably guessed, I chose the first." Lewis admitted that he imitated the meter of a Tennyson poem, worried that Smugy might therefore suspect a lack of invention, and made known his prepared defense, "I shall point out that Pope and Addison wrote all their poems in the same metre." After declaring Pope and Addison inferior poets to Horace, Lewis, only fifteen years old mind you, asks, "how can people advocate a 'modern education'? What could be better or more enjoyable than reading the greatest master-pieces of all time, under a man who has made them part of himself?"[6] To young Jack, the answer was nothing.

This sentiment in the "greatest masterpieces of all time" is important for understanding how young Jack thought. The classic works, reading, the life of escaping into great fictive worlds defined Lewis's most formative years. But Lewis didn't merely long to read great literature, as his many letters to his father show; he wanted people to talk to about them.

For the writer

Reading serves the writer well, when done in relationship. Talking about books, creating relationships based on reading accountability, and infusing current relationships with bookish sentiment—like Lewis did with his father—helps hone the writer's critical thinking about language and literature.

Do you have any "literary friendships"? What are your conversations with your literary friends like? Describe what makes them work. How have they affected your creativity? If you don't have a relationship like this, with whom could you begin one and how could you work to create it?

Do try: Set aside thirty minutes to think about and write on the importance of relationships and reading. Devote some time in thought before putting pen to page. When you start writing, focus on how reading can enliven a relationship and how relationships can enrich reading.

5. Ibid., 49.
6. Ibid.

6

What? You Too?

Lewis's readerly relationship with his father alerts us to an important intersection, where we're privy to the ways Lewis's reading life, personal relationships, and development as a writer meet. At this intersection we find the most revealing details of Lewis's formation as a writer. To walk down any one of these paths—what Lewis read, whom he conserved about literature with, and what he actually wrote—will usually lead you back onto the other two roads. Thus, reading Bunyan, "our own friend," as Lewis wrote to his father, becomes a trail that eventually leads to *The Pilgrim's Regress*, Lewis's first post-conversion attempt at authorship. We place Lewis's reading life in its truest context through this tripartite schema—his reading, relationships, and writing.

Among Lewis's literary relationships, none were more important than his lifelong friend Arthur Greeves. Lewis's relationship with Greeves is the very sum of a friendship built largely on and around reading and writing. That their friendship would be defined by this literary quality seems to have been fated from the beginning.

The Greeves family lived across the road from the Lewis family, though the two never came into contact until Greeves, laid up in bed sick, called for Lewis to visit. Greeves, often ill or convalescing, had called for Lewis to visit before, but Lewis, for one reason or another not interested enough in Greeves to take the time, had always ignored the requests. So it is interesting that Lewis would choose to visit Greeves the day he did.

Lewis recounts their fortuitous first meeting: "I found Arthur sitting up in bed. On the table beside him lay a copy of *Myths of the Norseman.*" Lewis asked, "do *you* like that?" Greeves asked, "do *you* like that?"

Lewis would later write in *The Four Loves*—and we can almost hear his first meeting with Greeves in these words—that

> Friendship arises out of mere Companionship when two or more of the companions discover that they have in common some insight or interest or even taste which the others do not share and which, till that moment, each believed to be his own unique treasure (or burden). The typical expression of opening Friendship would be something like, "What? You too? I thought I was the only one."[1]

Lewis discovered that he was, in fact, not the only one. In meeting Greeves, Lewis's relational and reading life converged and cross-pollinated. From that first companioned moment of common interest Greeves became both close friend and literary confidant. For Lewis, the two often overlapped. Lewis wrote to Greeves constantly and hardly ever without some mention of a new book. Comments by Lewis like, "I am deep in *Morte D-Arthur* by this time, and it is really the greatest thing I've ever read," thread through their letters.[2]

Reading permeated Jack's relationship with Arthur, and it gave them a special kind of discourse. Lewis fondly called Greeves, "Galahad," the fictional son of Lancelot and Elaine from Malory's *Le Morte d'Arthur*.[3] When asked by Greeves if he had ever been in love, Lewis gave quite the readerly answer:

> fool as I am, I am not quite such a fool as all that . . . though I have no personal experience of the thing they call, I have what is better—the experiences of Sapho, or Euripides of Catullus of Shakespeare or Spenser of Austen of Bronte of, of —anyone else I have read. We see through their eyes.[4]

Just as we can see his initial meeting with Greeves in Lewis's "What? You too?" treatment of friendship in *The Four Loves*, we can see in his answer to Greeves the seed of thought fully fleshed out in *An Experiment in Criticism*, when Lewis, discussing reading's power to provide escape, says,

---

1. Lewis, *The Four Loves*, 65.
2. Hooper, *Collected Letters* 1.104.
3. Ibid., 115. Lewis often began his letters to Arthur Greeves with, "Dear Galahad."
4. Ibid., 146.

My own eyes are not enough for me, I will see through those of others.[5]

One pair of eyes Lewis benefited from seeing through were those of A. C. Benson, author of *The Upton Letters*, a collection of essays in letter form written from a school master at "Upton College" to a sickly friend in Madeira, Portugal. Benson was an English essayist and the Master of Magdelene College, Cambridge, where Lewis would become Chair of Medieval and Renaissance Literature in 1954.

Lewis encountered Benson's *Upton Letters* at the age of sixteen, and from it had the "great revelation" that "we ought not to write about our actions but about our thoughts," an idea that he deems "wonderfully true." Lewis lamented to his father how

> we busy ourselves, you and I, telling each other about the weather and the little trivial happenings of each day, while the thoughts of our hearts, the really great experiences of our selves, are seldom spoken of.[6]

It is not hard to imagine how this revelation of writing about the inner life, the "thoughts of our hearts," might faintly foreshadow Lewis's characterization in *The Great Divorce*, a novel devoted to exposing the human condition. One might recall the conversation between the thin-voiced, quick-talking Ghost busily addressing the glorified Solid People. There on the very edge of Heaven, the superficial Ghost could only talk about such trivial happenings:

> Oh, my dear, I've had such a dreadful time, I don't know how I ever got here at all, I was coming with Elinor Stone and we'd arrange the whole thing and we were to meet at the corner of Sink Street; I made it perfectly plain because I knew what she was like and if I told her once I told her a hundred times I would not meet her outside that dreadful Marjoribanks woman's house, not after the way she'd treated me . . . that was one of the most dreadful things that happened to me . . . .[7]

Her soul hangs in the balance between eternal bliss and eternal woe, yet all the Ghost can do is ramble on about insignificant inconveniences. In creating a Ghost lost on the trivial happenings of her day, missing the

---

5. Lewis, *An Experiment in Criticism*, 140.

6. Hooper, *Collected Letters* 1.61.

7. Lewis, *The Great Divorce*, 75–76.

great experience of her self, perhaps Lewis returned to, perhaps even saw his story through, Benson.

For the writer

His introduction to Greeves marked the beginning of a new phase in Lewis's relational life. Their meeting also drastically changed his creative life. Relationally and creatively, Greeves brought him out of himself. His friendship with Greeves allowed him to see through eyes other than his own. The same holds true for any writer. Becoming a writer is largely about expanding the self, learning to see life through the eyes of those we know and what we read.

What kind of spiritual, emotional, or creative growth have relationships and reading brought you? How have you experienced life through another's eyes—either someone you know or something you've read? Why do you think our relationships—both to people and to books—are so influential in our lives?

Do try: Write about your relational and creative growth. Focus on one relationship or one book and how it has caused you to see through eyes other than your own. You don't have to keep to a particular structure. No thesis required. Just spend at least thirty minutes free-writing.

7

Tell Me More about John Silence

Books were what allowed Lewis to see with the eyes of others. Very often, Arthur Greeves's were also the ears through which he heard. Their friendship flourished by that shared question, "do *you* like that?" Their continual correspondence aerated Lewis's literary affection, full of exchanges like—

> I have here discovered an author exactly after my own heart, whom I am sure you would delight in, W. B. Yeats. He writes plays and poems or rare spirit and beauty about our old Irish mythology. I must really get my father to buy his books when I come home. His works have all got that strange, eerie feeling about them, of which we are both professed admirers. I must get hold of them, certainly.[1]

and

> I have started reading Homer's *Iliad.*[2]

Their friendship fostered in Lewis a habit of intellectual collaboration early in life. He delighted in sharing ideas about writing, literature, and language. In the Homer letter Lewis confesses his excitement at sharing *The Iliad*; struggling to "resist the temptation of telling you how stirring it is," he

---

1. Hooper, *Collected Letters* 1.59.
2. Ibid., 71.

wrote to Greeves, particularly stricken by "those fine, simple, euphonious lines, as they roll on with a roar like that of the ocean."[3]

Greeves gave ear to Lewis's maturing, increasingly keen criticism. Lewis found a friendly soundboard for his ripening literary reflections. He could ruminate in a letter and be assured of a friendly response. Each new book Lewis read and wrote to Greeves about offered him opportunity to form opinions about his close reading, articulate ideas about a poem's meter, or discuss an author's affect on his readers. In a letter from June 1916, Lewis shares a new literary find with Greeves, a novel by George Bernard Shaw called *Love among the Artists*.

> In odd moments last week I read an excellent novel by—you'd never guess—Bernard Shaw. . . . I wonder what the good author who takes his own works so seriously would think if he knew that he was read for pleasure to fill up the odd moments of a schoolboy.[4]

So much of what we know about Lewis's relationship to reading and writing—if and why he liked this book over another, how he judged the quality of an author's style, the ways a poem conjured a yearning for escape—lies in his reciprocity with Greeves. For Jack, hearing Arthur's thoughts on a book meant the heart of their friendship still beat. In the same Shaw letter, Lewis elicits responses from his dear friend:

> I think the whole gist of the thing, all about music, art etc. would appeal to you very strongly. Tell me if you do.

and

> If you go get the book, don't forget to read the preface which is very amusing.[5]

We've seen how collaborative an act reading was for Lewis, how he honed his ability to think and speak about literature through the community of reading. Earlier in this same letter, Lewis addressed a complaint from Greeves that some books grow "tiresome half way through."[6] Lewis knew very well what Greeves meant, but he shared a few exceptions: "'Phantastes',

---

3. Ibid., 71.
4. Ibid., 190.
5. Ibid.
6. Ibid., 189.

'Jane Eyre', 'Shirley' (which in fact only begins to get interesting about then) might be cited."[7] He then wrote to Greeves,

> tell me more about "John Silence" when you write, and also let me know the publisher and price, as I have forgotten again and may want it one of these days.[8]

Lewis followed that paragraph about books becoming tiresome halfway through reading them with another paragraph that begins,

> I don't like the way you say "don't tell anyone" that you thought "Frankenstein" badly written, and at once draw in your critical horns with the "of course I'm no judge" theory. Rot! You are a very good judge for me because your tastes run in the same direction. *And you ought to rely more on yourself than on anyone else in matters of books . . . .*[9]

Lewis offered his opinions on books with the same marked certainty he would go on to write books like *Miracles* and *Mere Christianity*. When it came to considering and critiquing books, Lewis trusted his instincts, and thought it important enough to the life of the man of letters that he insisted Greeves do the same. Admonishing Greeves to tell him about "John Silence" is a way to draw Greeves's literary spirit out. Lewis sought in Greeves a sharer of his imagination's intimacy, one devoted to the discourse of the written word.

For the writer

Writers have to learn to trust their instincts, to trust themselves in matters of books. Writers can't passively read books. They have to interrogate, scrutinize, and celebrate them. Writers form judgments about what they read, and they have to trust those judgments. For the writer to rely on herself is to awaken that internal literary critic. This is part of the writer's task: to engage literature with an active mind and sense of conviction about what the writing does and does not achieve.

---

7. Ibid.

8. Ibid.

9. Ibid., 189–90. *Emphasis mine.*

What are your favorite books? Why? What makes them good? What about your least favorite? Why didn't you like them? What are your criteria for judging?

Do try: Write a 750–1,000 review of any book of your choice. Be detailed and decisive in your opinions, but make sure to support them with evidence from the text. End your piece with a recommendation—or non-recommendation—of the book.

8

Avoid Nearly All Magazines

Long after Lewis had become famous, he received a letter from a seventh-grade school girl named Thomasine who was given the assignment to write to her favorite author. She was to ask his advice on becoming a writer. Though Lewis begins his advice to young Thomasine with, "it is very hard to give any general advice on writing," he goes on to offer eight recommendations. The second point (to the other seven bits of advice we'll turn later) he passed onto Thomasine was,

> Read all the good books you can, and avoid nearly all magazines.[1]

An important lesson on writing, preceded only by the advice to "turn off the radio," Lewis indeed read all the good books he could. We are also safe in presuming that he avoided popular magazines! Lewis faithfully kept his own advice.

A good example is his, "Who is Elizabeth Taylor?" That was Lewis's response when, in discussing the differences between "prettiness" and "beauty," Lewis biographer and editor Walter Hooper suggested, "Miss Taylor was a great beauty."

Hooper further suggested to Lewis, "If you read the newspapers, you would know who she is," to which Lewis responded, "Ah-h-h-h! But that is how I keep myself 'unspotted from the world.'" Lewis insisted that if

---

1. Hooper, *Collected Letters* 3.1108.

Hooper had to read the newspapers he "have a frequent 'mouthwash' with *The Lord of the Rings* or some other great book."[2]

To help read all the good books he could, Lewis was well advised. He entered the tutelage of W. T. Kirkpatrick in 1914. Kirkpatrick—the "Great Knock" as Lewis, and his brother and father before, both also Kirkpatrick's pupils, called him—was as close to being a "purely logical entity" as Lewis would ever meet. Lewis recalls arriving at the Knock's house on a Saturday and being told he would begin Homer on Monday. When Monday came, Kirkpatrick opened Book I of *The Iliad* and began to read.[3] Such was Lewis's life under the Knock. Under Kirkpatrick, Lewis read widely, nimbly holding the works of several authors in mind and discussing them comparatively:

> I have been devoting this week to the reading of *Othello*, which I like as well as any Shakespearian play I have read. . . . But then of course Shakespeare at his best always works on titanic lines, and the vices and virtues of Lear, Macbeth, Hamlet, Othello, Desdemona, etc., are magnified to a pitch more splendid and terrible than anything in real life.[4]

Kirkpatrick brought Lewis into the high green countries of new creativity. Once, when Lewis was away in Belfast for an eight-week stay, Kirkpatrick spurred Lewis to spend read vast volumes of classic literature:

> I suggest you order . . . the following; Plato: *The Phaedo*, if you have it. Demosthenes: *De Corona*. Tacitus: *The Annals*. Aeschlus: *The Agamemnon*. . . . I expect you are browsing at present on the pastures of general literature, and this of course is as it should be. If however you find English too easy and sigh for more worlds to conquer, I recommend the perusal of any German book you may happen to come across.[5]

This intense time of reading produced a burst of new writing. While in Belfast, somewhere between Plato and Tacitus, Lewis wrote and added six poems to a notebooked collection of fifty-two poems he called *Metrical Meditations of a Cod*.

---

2. Hooper, "Introduction," *Present Concerns*, 7.

3. Lewis, *Surprised by Joy*, 140.

4. Ibid., 132.

5. Hooper, *Collected Letters* 1.141.

C. S. Lewis and the Art of Writing

For the writer

That a writer be an avid reader is vitally important. *What* the writer reads is as important. Lewis had little use for ephemeral journalism, magazine writing, writing untested by time. Good writers, realizing how creative input affects creative output, read good literature.

What kinds of writing do you most read? Magazines? Poems? Short stories? Novels? What are some of the differences between the quality of writing in an acclaimed novel and a popular magazine article? How does reading good literature influence your writing differently than reading bad literature?

Do try: In 300 words, write about the ways reading good literature sponsors good writing. Feel free to use a specific example of how something you read fostered your writing.

9

Phantastes

Lewis burgeoned in the intellectual life. New books became new discoveries. When looking for moments of literary significance, we see in his letters a chronicle of exhilarated literary moments that indelibly impressed themselves on his creativity. One moment of lasting influence came with George MacDonald's *Phantastes*.

In March of 1916, Lewis wrote to Greeves to announce,

> I have had a great literary experience this week. I have discovered yet another author to add to our circle—our very own set: never since I first read "The well at the world's end" have I enjoyed a book so much—and indeed I think my new "find" is quite as good as Malory or Morris himself. The book, to get to the point, is George MacDonald's "Faerie Romance," *Phantastes* . . . .[1]

To compare this newfound *Phantastes* with the likes of Malory or Morris's *The Well at the World's End* was high praise, indeed.

Lewis considered Malory that rare where-have-you-been-all-my-life kind of author. Upon first reading Malory, Lewis wrote to Greeves—or "Galahad," knight of the Round Table and Malory protagonist, as Lewis dubbed him—to announce the experience as life changing:

---

1. Hooper, *Collected Letters* 1.169.

> Do you ever wake up in the morning and suddenly wonder why
> you have not bought such-and-such a book long ago, and then
> decided that life without it will be quite unbearable?[2]

In this same letter, Lewis pointed out to Greeves that there is a con-
nection between Malory and Morris. It was Malory from whom Morris
"copied the style of his prose Tales."[3] And with Morris's prose, Lewis had
already fallen in love.

A precociously keen reader, Lewis thought carefully about a text's
style and themes. Lewis admired both in Morris's writing. As a teenager,
Lewis was utterly and unabashedly enthralled by the fantastic and the faery
in literature. It was the lack of those elements that caused him to criticize
Morris's *The Roots of the Mountains*, reporting to Greeves that he was "des-
perately disappointed to find that there is nothing, supernatural, faery or
unearthly in it at all."[4] Morris's *Well at the World's End* was another matter.
Lewis loved the novel and found in Morris a kindred mind. Morris's writing
brought to mind the Belfast world of his childhood, and his and Arthur
Greeves's "lovely hill-walk in the frost and fog."[5] Morris wrote the kinds of
stories that Lewis had longed for since he read Beatrix Potter and Siegfried,
those stories saturated in a sense of otherness. Lewis read and reread *Well
at the World's End*—he maintained a lifelong belief that a signature trait of
the literary was not their reading but their rereading of a book—and found
the book's appeal greater over time:

> I have been reading again "The Well at the World's End," and it has
> completely ravished me. There is something awfully nice about
> reading a book again, with all the unconscious memories it brings
> back.[6]

To Lewis, Morris's *Well* performed the work of recovery and escape:
the recovery of the green-fogged downs of a childhood world and an escape
into the one beyond.[7]

2. Ibid., 94.

3. Ibid.

4. Ibid., 122.

5. Ibid., 153.

6. Ibid.

7. To borrow from Tolkien's "On Faerie Stories," where Tolkien gives four of Faerie's
functions: escape, recovery, consolation, and fantasy.

After *Well at the World's End*, Lewis read all the Morris he could find, likening reading Morris to his earlier encounter with Wagner, who brought him that transcendent expanse of Northernness. As with Wagner, reading Morris worked powerfully on Lewis:

> the growth of the new delight is marked by my sudden realization, almost with a sense of disloyalty, that the letters WILLIAM MORRIS were coming to have at least as potent a magic in them as Wagner.[8]

So when Lewis says that not since he first read *The Well at the World's End* had he enjoyed a book as much as *Phantastes*, and when he claims discovering MacDonald quite as good as Malory or Morris, he says a quite lot.

Terentianus Maurus, second-century Latin grammarian, wrote *pro captu lectoris, habent sua fata libelli* (according to the capacity of the reader, books have their destinies).[9] No book ever found its destiny in the hands of a reader with a higher capacity than George MacDonald's *Phantastes* found in the hands of C. S. Lewis. In few instances in his life is the impact of reading more apparent on his writing than in Lewis's first exposure to MacDonald.

Lewis haphazardly ran across MacDonald's "Faerie Romance" in a bookstall, and shortly after, insisted that Greeves "simply MUST" get the book at once.[10] Despite the first chapter's "conventional faery tale style" and its inclusion of a couple of "shockingly bad" poems, *Phantastes* offered Lewis a heroic journey into faery. MacDonald brought Lewis into a new country, one that, strangely enough, seemed like the "old country" first visited in works by English epic poet Edmund Spenser, Irish poet W. B. Yeats, and of course, Sir Thomas Malory and William Morris. The experience was uncanny. "For the first time," Lewis wrote, "the song of the sirens sounded like the voice of my mother of my nurse."[11] MacDonald called into all Lewis had known, bringing voices "from the world's end" to his side, in his room, in his body, and behind him, as he describes it.[12]

Phantastes cast a bright shadow of Holiness. In reading MacDonald's faery romance, Lewis welcomed holiness into his real world. While Lewis

---

8. Lewis, *Surprised by Joy*, 164.

9. Terentianus, *De Litteris Syllabis*, verse 1286.

10. Hooper, *Collected Letters* 1.170.

11. Lewis, *Surprised by Joy*, 179.

12. Ibid., 179–80.

admits that MacDonald, if measured by the quality of his writing alone, writes with an undistinguished, fumbling, verbose style, his stories still possess a mythopoeic power, an ability to incarnate spiritual truth in story and then pass that truth on to the reader.[13] It was MacDonald's mythopoeia that caused Lewis to proclaim that *Phantastes* had baptized his imagination.[14] The gravity of MacDonald's writing gives weight to several themes in Lewis's most important works. The influence of MacDonald's titular character from *Lilith* shows up in Lewis's Narnia Chronicles. He disperses MacDonald's quotes throughout *The Problem of Pain*. MacDonald is to Lewis in *The Great Divorce* what Virgil is to Dante in *The Inferno*. It's in *The Great Divorce*, published thirty years after discovering *Phantastes*, that we find MacDonald doing in fiction what he did in life, guiding Lewis into deeper truth.

Lewis edited an anthology of selections from MacDonald's works and in the preface confessed,

> I have never concealed the fact that I regarded him as my master; indeed I fancy I have never written a book in which I did not quote from him.[15]

For the writer

Writers are debtors to those books that baptized their imaginations. Reading deeply of a favorite author's works, allowing a beloved book's bright shadow to set in, and even writing about a book's or author's influence forms a sense of creative heritage in the writer. Good writers know—and in a myriad of ways carry on the literary legacy of—their masters.

What exactly do you think Lewis might have meant when he said that MacDonald's writing baptized his imagination? Has any book come close to "baptizing" your imagination? What authors do you go to for inspiration and creative nourishment?

---

13. Lewis, "Preface," *George MacDonald*, xxxii–xxxiii.

14. Ibid., 181.

15. Lewis, "Preface," *George MacDonald: An Anthology*, xxxvii; George MacDonald's *Diary of an Old Soul* found Lewis at the right time and continued to form him. Lewis would call MacDonald his master. "He seems to know everything and I find my own experience in it constantly . . . ." Lewis liked the "homespun quality" of MacDonald's work, comparing it to Herbert.

Do try: Write a reflection on how an idea or theme from a work of literature can so powerfully transform someone. Feel free to be personal or theoretical in your approach. If you like, aim at the influence an idea from literature can have on a writer's philosophy of or approach to writing. No length requirement. Just write.

IO

Like a Thunderclap

The biggest shaking up I've got from a book, since I first read *Phantastes*—

So Lewis said to Arthur Greeves about Jacob Boehme's *The Signature of All Things*. Like Malory, Morris, and MacDonald before, Boehme, a German Christian mystic, made an impression on the aspiring writer. *The Signature of All Things* deals with what is known as the law of signatures, a fundamental law of magic that holds to the hidden meaning within every physical object. The idea impressed Lewis:

> It is not such a pleasant experience as *Phantastes*, and if it continues to give me the same feeling when I understand more I shall give it up. No fooling about for me: and I keep one hand firmly gripped around the homely & simple things. But it is a real book: i.e. it's not like a book at all, but like a thunderclap. Heaven defend us—what things there are knocking about the world![1]

Lewis tells Greeves that he had two "quite distinct experiences in reading" Boehme. The first was syntactical: "Certain sentences moved and excited me although I couldn't understand them." And the second, phenomenological, as Lewis had "at certain points a feeling of distress, and even of horror."[2]

---

1. Hooper, *Collected Letters* 1.859.
2. Ibid.

As it turned out, Lewis encountered in *Signature* something more spiritually substantial than his eroding atheism could comfortably handle.

In prose and thought, Boehme represented a new paradigm, a vision of reality more solid than Lewis had so far known. Something of that reality made its way into Lewis's prose. Boehme's poignant syntax and themes of spiritual life stayed with Lewis, as he continued to mull over Boehme's writing, finding the "most lovely sentences" full of the kind of self-emptying tropes on which later books like *The Problem of Pain*, *The Great Divorce*, and *Mere Christianity* would run. Taken by the quality of writing in *The Signature of All Things*, Lewis transcribed Boehme's most moving sentences to Greeves:

> That many a twig withers on the tree is not the tree's fault, for it withdraws its sap from no twig, only the twig gives forth itself too eagerly with the desire: it runs on in self will, it is taken by the inflammation of the sun and the fire, before it can draw sap again in its mother and refresh itself.[3]

> He breaks self-hood as a vessel wherein he lies captive, and buds forth continually in God's will-spirit, with his desire regained in God, as a fair blossom springs out of the earth.[4]

Books like Boehme's left craters in Lewis's creativity. Auspicious authors found an inviting reader in Lewis, and while few authors approached the kind of importance a MacDonald or Boehme held in Lewis's life, many were given the chance. In seeking out new volumes to read, Lewis didn't just scour the bookstalls, as he had done when he found the gem of *Phantastes*. He invited new titles from those he corresponded with, and again, none was more important in his literary relationships than Arthur Greeves.

In a 1916 letter, Lewis wrote—somewhat foreshadowing his announcement of his later conversion by the help of literary friends—to declare the benefits of taking Greeves' reading advice:

> I am now—by the same post—writing for a book called "British Ballads" (Everyman) in the chocolate binding of which I used to disapprove: so you see I am gradually converted to all your views. Perhaps one of these days you may even make a Christian of me.[5]

---

3. Ibid., 863; Boehme, *The Signature of All Things*, 219.

4. Ibid.; ibid., 203.

5. Hooper, *Collected Letters* 1.171.

Greeves had a tremendous influence on Lewis's reading life. From the novel *The Life and Opinions of Tristam Shandy, Gentleman* by Laurence Sterne, to the works of Jane Austen, Lewis loved to banter with him about the books he was reading, conversing about an author's style or merit. No books were beyond consideration, and another's recommendations were never lost on Lewis, as he said, "one often learns to appreciate a book through one's friends in this way."[6] Again, to Arthur Greeves, Lewis complained in 1918, "you don't tell me what you are reading: always remember that it keeps us in touch."

Greeves suggested new books to Lewis, each received with appropriation and a degree of enthusiasm. So Lewis's tastes for literature grew, as did the sophistication of those tastes.

Good writers are good readers because good readers keep their ears tuned to language. Before he was twenty, Lewis already had a masterful ear for the sound of words. Quoting a work from poet Philip Francis Little's collection *Thermopylae and Other Poems*, Lewis wrote his father in celebration of the poetry's melody, the lines' "masterly phrasing and gorgeous imagery!"[7] No doubt due to years of poetic practice, Lewis developed an ear for fine language, pointing out phrases like the "golden brawn" of the sunrise, the "various viands" of the rainbow, and the "gorgeous, great, gratuitous" realities of nature.

We see Lewis's sensitivity to words smattered throughout his later writings. Books like *Studies in Words*, with its scholarly scrutiny of word meaning and usage, and essays like "The Language of Religion," with its parsing between ordinary, scientific, and poetic language, show a writer attuned to language's use and euphony. Those hours reading the likes of Philip Francis Little, Spenser, Homer, and Boehme honed Lewis into a writer apt to adopt language that conveyed

> to us the quality of experiences which we have not had, or perhaps can never have, to use factors within our experience so that they become pointers to something outside our experience.[8]

---

6. Ibid., 332.

7. Ibid., 172. Lewis quotes, "Oh, wave! Thy clemency is open/To shrewd suspicion."

8. Ibid., 321; Lewis, "The Language of Religion," 177.

For the writer

A love for language underpins the act of writing. A book's idea is only as powerful as the language that conveys it. Writers that glean from both a book's syntax and subject help cultivate their craft. To know why a sentence sounds beautiful, or doesn't convey the idea it's meant to convey, or why comes across like a thunderclap, the writer must become a student of language, learning to love its intricacies and eager to explore its possibilities.

What are a few examples of beautiful writing? What makes those examples beautiful? How do you know a good, evocative, or powerful sentence when you read it? What makes the language in those sentences so effective?

Do try: In no more than 500 words, write about the most powerful, beautiful, moving passage in literature that you can think of. Provide an explanation for what makes that passage so poignant. Be specific in the points you make. And of course, write this prompt with language worthy its topic.

II

A Great Reading Event

When Lewis finally arrived at Oxford, his reading life both broadened and deepened. Now an Oxford man, a new intellective world surrounded him. Here Lewis met many whose breadth of knowledge of modern literature vastly eclipsed his own, those who made him "feel how deep is my ignorance of modern, that is to say, contemporary, literature, especially poetry."[1]

Lewis often found himself in a state of "amazed silence amid glib talk" of twentieth-century poets, but stayed in the solace of older works, safeguards against the deadly "crazes" that "arise so easily about a new writer."[2]

Even when the rumblings and reality of World War I disrupted his life, Lewis found refuge in reading. After a recent move to an Officers' Command Depot in the little coast town of Eastbourne, Lewis read and eagerly reported to Greeves the pleasures of a Browning biography, a work depicting "just what the life of a writer should be," which led him to read Browning's *Paracelsus*.

In this same 1918 letter to Greeves, Lewis reveals a great deal about his life as reader and writer at the time. After mentioning Browning, Lewis announces a great reading event: learning to enjoy Shakespeare! Lewis bought an "Everyman" edition of Shakespeare's Comedies and just finished

---

1. Hooper, *Collected Letters* 1.342.
2. Ibid.

Measure for Measure.[3] We see the fruit of this great reading event in an essay like, "Hamlet: The Prince or The Poem?"

If in 1918, Lewis was a Bard beginner, by 1942, when he first delivered the "Prince or The Poem" at the Annual Shakespeare Lecture of the British Academy, he was an interpretive virtuoso, speaking as sharply on Shakespeare as he did on any author. In "Prince or The Poem," Lewis acknowledges, "Shakespeare offered me a King who could not even sentence a man to banishment without saying":

> The sly slow hours shall not determine
> The dateless limit of thy dear exile.[4]

Left to himself, Lewis says, he would have taken these lines as how "beautiful, willful, passionate, unfortunate kings killed long ago ought to talk." But the critic in Lewis's ear, he admits, dripped a kind of readerly poison, persuading him that he "ought to prize such words chiefly as illustrations of what he [the critic] called Richard's weakness, and (worse still) inviting me to admire the vulgar, bustling efficiency of Bolingbroke."[5] The critics gave the same interpretation to thousands, an interpretation that closed the book of Shakespeare to Lewis for years. Lewis just couldn't read Shakespeare in the critic's way.

Here Lewis offers a lesson in close reading. He attributes his matured understanding of Shakespeare to his broad reading life. "Only much later," Lewis writes,

> reinforced with a wider knowledge of literature, and able now to rate at its value the humble little outfit of prudential maxims which really underlay much of the talk about Shakespeare's characters, did I return and read him with enjoyment.[6]

The critical conclusion—a conclusion Lewis came to by reading others' similar conclusions—was

> to surrender oneself to the poetry and the situation. It is only through them that you can reach the characters, and it is for their sake that the characters exist.[7]

3. Ibid., 418.

4. Lewis, "Hamlet: The Prince or The Poem?" 58; Shakespeare, *King Richard I1.* 1.3.150–51.

5. Lewis, "Hamlet: The Prince or The Poem?" 58.

6. Ibid.

7. Ibid., 59.

Lewis said in *An Experiment in Criticism* that the literary reader *receives* a text, while the unliterary only *uses* it. Right reading is a matter of surrender.

The first inclination of the receptive reader isn't to ridicule, but to reap. To glean all that the poetry will bear:

> Interpretations which compel you to read their speeches with a certain superiority, to lend then a note of "insincerity," to strive in any way against their beauty, are self-condemned. Poets do not make beautiful verse in order to have it "guyed." ... For the poetry, the clothes, and the stance are the substance; the character "as it would have to be in real life" is only a shadow.[8]

The reader who puts poetry to the test of real-life repugnance misses the point. Poetry's beauty is the substance. To Lewis, the "sly slow hours shall not determine" is both the style and its own substance. In "Prince or The Poem," we find a familiar culmination. Lewis's first experiences with a book are usually resurrected in a later experience with that same text. So it went with Shakespeare. Lewis's literary week in 1918 when he learned to enjoy Shakespeare found a kind of consummation in 1942, in his argument for the enjoyment of reading Shakespeare.

It's also in this 1918 letter to Greeves that Lewis announces a return to writing after an inactive season interned in hospitals and camps. Along with acquiring a taste for the Bard, Lewis comments, "at the same time I am doing a lot of writing again. I have just finished a short narrative," a poetic version of a work Lewis began in 1916 called *Dymer*.

For the writer

Reading requires intellectual honesty. Even C. S. Lewis—one of the most well-read writers of the twentieth century—found himself under-read in modern poetry. He initially struggled with Shakespeare. There were times when he had to beat his head against some kinds of literature to understand it. The reading act was so meaningful to him because he learned to receive the text, rather than master or use the text. It's the reader's first job to submit to the text, to surrender to its story and the beauty of its language.

---

8. Ibid.

What kind of reader would you say you are? Do you actively engage a book by allowing it to work deeply in your intellect and imagination? What does it mean to receive the text?

Do try: Choose a short work of literature—short story, essay, or poem—and write 450–500 words on your reading process. Touch on what you first notice, what you most value, what you have difficulty understanding, and what resonates most deeply. Evaluate how you read.

12

Conscious of Style

The way Lewis writes about reading Morris, or MacDonald, or learning to enjoy Shakespeare depicts the reading life as a series of epiphanies. And for Lewis, it was. After reading H. G. Wells' novel *Marriage*, Lewis announced to Greeves,

> It opens new landscapes to me—how one felt that on finding that a new kind of book was waiting for one, in the old days—and I have decided to read more of his serious books. It is funny that I—and perhaps you—read the old books for pleasure and always turn to contemporaries with the notion of "improving my mind." With most, I fancy, the direct opposite is so.[1]

The epitome of an active reader, Lewis thought intently about what and why he read. He privileged reading for pleasure, distinguishing it from reading meant to improve the mind. He ably gleaned the fruit of substance from some books and the signature of style from others. I am glad you like the *Lives of the Poets*, Lewis wrote to his brother in 1928,

> there is no subject on which more nonsense has been talked than the style of Johnson. For me his best sentences in writing have the same feeling as his best conversation—"pop! it was so sudden." I don't know anyone who can settle a thing so well in half a dozen words.[2]

1. Hooper, *Collected Letters* 1.472.
2. Ibid., 772.

Conversational style and concision. It's perhaps these two elements that best characterize Lewis's own writing. Little doubt that Lewis developed a love for that style because he first found it attractive in his reading.

There exists, to use Lewisian terms, a great divorce between literary and unliterary readers. In *An Experiment in Criticism*, Lewis gives five characteristics of unliterary readers, that is to say, those readers who merely want to "use" literature, to understand it quickly and extract the words' nearest meaning. Rather than be receptive of the beauty and complexity of the "sound and sense" of language, as the literary reader is, the unliterary reader judges a book by its utility.[3] Lewis describes unliterary readers as:

1. those who avoid the literary for the periodical, like the daily news

2. those who have no ear for language, who read exclusively by the eye

3. those unconscious of style, to the point of favoring bad writing over good literature

4. those who enjoy unsophisticated narrative

5. those who demand a fast pace, adventurous plot

Lewis discusses reading here, but in *An Experiment in Criticism*, he has in mind both sides of the literary act, the nature of reading a text and the quality of what it is that's being read—the writing of the text. Virtually every page of *Experiment in Criticism* has the subtext, "writers take heed," with warnings against bad writing nestled in Lewis's warnings against bad reading.

Lewis first describes the unliterary's inclination to read ephemeral periodicals instead of timeless texts. Choosing the daily news over Dostoevsky is a sign of the unread, rather than the relevant, reader. There are in Lewis's characteristics of bad reading the threads of insensitivity to language. Note the bad reader's—and, Lewis will later add, the bad writer's—deafness to the sound of language. No accounting for words' musicality with unliterary types. The bad reader has a distinct disregard for style and the story's sophistication. There is also the matter of the unliterary's exaggerated expectation that literature should only thrill.

After Lewis's close friend and fellow Inkling Charles Williams died in 1945, Lewis started to work on an anthology of essays in his honor. Lewis called his contribution "On Stories," and one of its themes is the dichotomy between the literary and unliterary reader. Some of the lines along which

---

3. Lewis, *An Experiment in Criticism*, 28–30.

Lewis parsed these distinctions include the unliterary's inordinate need for excitement in a book's plot:

> If to love Story is to love excitement then I ought to be the greatest lover of excitement alive. But the fact is that what is said to be the most "exciting" novel in the world, *The Three Musketeers*, makes no appeal to me at all. The total lack of atmosphere repels me.[4]

A reliance on mere emotional affect over the work of the imagination:

> it is very difficult to tell in any given case whether a story is piercing to the unliterary reader's deeper imagination or only exciting his emotions. You cannot tell even by reading the story for yourself. Its badness proves very little. The more imagination the reader has, being an untrained reader, the more he will do for himself.[5]

And a misguided belief that reading a book once makes for a literary life:

> An unliterary man may be defined as one who reads books once only. There is hope for a man who has never read Malory or Boswell or Tristram Shandy or Shakespeare's *Sonnets*: but what can you do with a man who says he "has read" them, meaning he has read them once, and thinks that this settles the matter.[6]

For the writer

Reading isn't a monolithic act, and approaches to reading aren't all equal. The reader's taste, consciousness of style, use of the imagination, and appreciation for a book's language determines how literary the reading experience is. Active reading, the kind of reading that aims to receive rather than use a text, opens new landscapes to the reader.

What are the differences between a literary and an unliterary reader? In what ways are you a literary reader? Or, an unliterary? How does the way you read affect the way you write?

Do try: In 500 words, explore the correlation between being a literary—or unliterary reader—and writing. Begin by theorizing how being a literary or unliterary reader influences the quality of one's writing. Support each idea with evidence.

4. Lewis, "On Stories," 7.
5. Ibid., 16.
6. Ibid.

13

Imagination and Mere Fancy

Those five characteristics of an unliterary reader from *An Experiment in Criticism*—avoiding the literary, reading only with the eye, unconscious of style, enjoying the unsophisticated story, and demanding a fast plot—show us just how judicious a reader Lewis was. To Lewis, reading meant the thoughtful, reflective, discriminating reception of writing. He adopted these beliefs about reading honestly over years of deliberate practice, years and years of living in literature going back to his home library of Little Lea. Lewis read referentially, continually evaluating one book by another he had read, and often, enjoyed better, always assuming the role of critic.

Upon reading *Water Babies* by Christian children's writer Charles Kingsley, Lewis comparatively referred to works by MacDonald—think *Phantastes*—after whose work Kingsley's is "tasteless."[1] The difference between Kingsley's and MacDonald's is that between a good and a very good book. Kingsley's story brought mere fancy, while in MacDonald one finds the imaginative. "Put the two side by side," Lewis wrote, "and see how imagination differs from mere fancy, and holiness from mere morality."[2]

Lewis drew his notions of fancy and imagination from another important text he read during his time at Oxford, Samuel Taylor Coleridge's *Biographia Literaria*.[3]

1. Hooper, *Collected Letters* 1.901.
2. Ibid.
3. Lewis first wrote about Coleridge's *Biographia Literaria* with friend and fellow

In *Biographia*, Coleridge describes fancy as a mechanical operation of the mind, an accumulation of dazzling data. Fancy is a lesser imagination. Rather than create, fancy merely imitates. It works with memory and empirical evidence. Imagination, though, has a "mysterious power" and deals in the hidden spiritual meanings within the data. To Coleridge, the *primary* imagination is the finite mind's repetition "of the eternal act of creation in the infinite I am."[4] *Secondary* imagination, according to Coleridge, is an echo of the primary imagination in lesser degree. An imagination that "dissolves, diffuses, dissipates, in order to re-create . . . yet still at all events it struggles to idealize and to unify." Coleridge esteemed fancy below the secondary imagination. Void of the metaphysically meaningful, fancy deals only in fixities and definites, and it was fancy that Lewis discerned in Kingsley. While Kingsley mustered up a moral tale, MacDonald wrote with the solid substance of transcendent holiness.

MacDonald rounded out Lewis's thinking about the imagination more than any other author. MacDonald held imagination as "that faculty in man which is likest to the prime operation of the power of God."[5] Imagination is man's chief creative power, itself "made in the image of the imagination of God."[6]

What the imagination is and how it is used occupied Lewis's thinking on creativity and the writing act. He returned to and conversed about the imagination throughout his life. In 1955, Dorothy Sayers—mystery writer, friend, and author of *The Mind of the Maker*—corresponded with Lewis about fantasy and the imagination and claimed that the writer's imagination indiscriminately included any material exposed to it:

> I think the trouble is that the unscrupulous old ruffian inside one who does the actual writing doesn't care tuppence where he gets his raw material from. Fantasy, memory, observation, odds and ends of reading, and sheer invitations are all grist to his mill, and he mixes everything up together regardless.[7]

---

poetry lover, Leo Baker, in 1920 and referred to the work regularly. Cf. Hooper, *Collected Letters* 1.507–8.

4. Coleridge, *The Biographia Literaria*, XVIII.

5. MacDonald, "The Imagination: Its Functions and Its Culture," 3.

6. Ibid., 4.

7. Hooper, *Collected Letters* 3.683. See fn. 370.

To which Lewis replied, in the dichotomous vein of Coleridge, that the imagination meant more than a mental mixture and had to be defined in several ways, starting with,

> The mere image-making faculty, the "mind's eye" (also its nose, ear etc.) wh[ich] ought to be called imagination if we literary meddlers hadn't spoiled that word for its plain sense.[8]

After Lewis's conversion to Christianity, imagination's plain sense, the human faculty for making images, began to carry spiritual significance. The imaginative mind, like the good book, found purpose in life's ultimate purpose, to draw the soul further out of itself: "almost the main work of life is to come out of our selves, out of the little, dark prison we are all born in."[9]

For the writer

Above all, reading is an imaginative act. A good book pours the material of the imagination into the reader's world while transporting into another. The imagination requires exercise. Readers must search for those books that brim with the imagination, and discern those that only meddle in mere fancy. The reader has to experience the imagination continually to grow in appreciation for and appropriation of it. Imaginative books find their full potential in the hands of imaginative readers.

What books have most exercised your imagination? Has your imaginative capacity grown? How so? What has that growth looked like in your creative life and writing?

Do try: Write a work of imaginative flash fiction. Create characters, plot, setting, and a story arc. The length shouldn't exceed 1,000 words. Your chief aim is high imagination. Be creative. Be bold.

8. Ibid.
9. Ibid., 759.

14

Pleased to Find Keats

Reading, talking books, and writing placed Lewis in a coveted intellectual community. Surrounded by literary readers and talented writers, "removed from the common mob," Lewis felt perfectly content.[1] Oxford meant the beginning of a life spent in literature. Oxford friend and English scholar Nevill Coghill recalls the kind of life in letters he and Lewis hoped for:

> We saw clearly what lay before us, a life of reading and teaching, perhaps of writing—for, as we confessed to each other very soon, we both hoped to be poets, or at least writers.[2]

What lay before Lewis was much the same as what lay behind. His saturated reading life had suited him for the life ahead. Oxford would require a sharp readerly mind, prepared by Lewis's innumerable impromptu criticisms.

"The book itself is a glorious feast," wrote Lewis to Greeves after reading Philip Sidney's *Arcadia*:

> I don't know how to explain its particular charm, because it is not at all like anything I ever read before: and yet in places like all of them.[3]

1. Hooper, *Collected Letters* 1.288. More than once Lewis reminded Greeves of their earlier days sending and receiving their writing. Cf. *Collected Letters* 1.323.

2. Coghill, "The Approach to English," 53.

3. Hooper, *Collected Letters* 1.196.

Not all criticism can be so kind, of course, and Lewis sharpened his critical tongue when a book gave him occasion. Recalling a rainy day he spent indoors reading an unnamed modern novel, Lewis once wrote to Greeves,

> I have read nothing lately, except a foolish modern novel which I read at one sitting—or rather one lying on the sofa, this afternoon in the middle of a terrible thunderstorm. I think, that if modern novels are to be read at all, they should be taken like this, at one gulp, and then thrown away—preferably into the fire . . . .[4]

Lewis thought books should be judged with a measure of certainty, and he received every book he read—to say nothing of the modern literature he so famously disliked—with rare critical awareness. Greeves once mentioned a book to Lewis titled *Literary Taste: How to Form It*, to which Lewis responded, ". . . the edition is pretty but the book is not of any value."[5]

The idea that you could learn literature the "way you learn golf" was ludicrous to Lewis. And what of the author of *Literary Taste*, novelist and journalist Arnold Bennett? A "priggish hack."[6] Lewis saw the kind of culture that would produce a book like *Literary Taste* as no less than anathema. Upon finding a series called Lubbock's *Hundred Best Books*—or "HUNDRED BEST BOOKS!!!" as Lewis put it—he wrote to his brother, Warnie,

> How I abominate such culture for the many, such tastes ready made, such standardization of the brain. To substitute for the infinite wandering of the true reader thro' the byways of the country he discovers, a char-a-banc tour.[7]

Everything about a collection like Lubbock's went against Lewis's philosophy of reading. Since childhood, Lewis's reading life was a free exploration of imaginative worlds and vast vistas of ideas. A culture that reduced reading to arbitrary prescriptive categorization, that emptied the act of reading of its awe, proved useless to Jack.

Given what we've seen of Lewis's definitive druthers in all things literary, it might not come as a surprise that Lewis also formed opinions of people based on the authors they read. During his early days at University College, Oxford, when Lewis had just begun to meet people, he wrote that

4. Ibid., 202.
5. Ibid., 240.
6. Ibid.
7. Ibid., 581.

he was "pleased to find Keats, Shelley, Oscar Wilde, Dante & Villon, as well as Plutarch & one of the lately executed Sinn Fein poets," upon meeting the eventually distinguished lawyer Theobald Butler.[8] To Lewis, the books an acquaintance kept in his library became a means of introduction.

Lewis's time at Oxford saw his reading and writing intersect in mutually fostering ways. We've seen how certain books stayed with Lewis, planting ideas in his creative consciousness. And some stories, like Apuleius's tale of Cupid and Psyche in *The Golden Ass*, took deep roots, growing for years to come.[9] Lewis would retell Apuleius's myth in arguably his finest work of literary fiction, his 1956 novel *Till We Have Faces*.

Early in his publishing career, when feelings of frustration were more frequent than success, Lewis found consolation in reading. "If only I could get my book [*Spirits in Bondage*] accepted," Lewis wrote to Greeves, "it would give me a tremendous fillip and take my mind off the future."[10] The only comfort Lewis knew in this time of waiting was fantasy of a familiar author—"In my present mood few things have pleased me more than MacDonald's 'The Golden and the Princess' . . . ."[11]

For the writer

Literary reading—the active reception of books that Lewis practiced—includes criticism as well as praise. Some books are received as glorious feasts, others as of no value. The active reader trusts his judgment to discern the former from the latter. The active reader, whether he is pleased to find Keats or unfortunate to run across a priggish hack, develops openness to genuine literary experiences that should result in the freedom to judge a book's merit.

How do you grow a critical eye for literature? What role does culture play in forming one's literary tastes? What does your inner critic value and devalue in a work of literature?

Do try: If you had to choose three virtues that characterized literary criticism, what would they be? Write an essay defining the task of literary

8. Ibid., 303.
9. Ibid., 304.
10. Ibid., 393.
11. Ibid.

criticism based on your three virtues. You create these virtues. An example would be: Literary criticism's three chief virtues guide the critic to judge a work of literature by 1) its ability to stir the imagination, 2) the clarity of its writing, and 3) its ability to convey timeless, counter-cultural truths. Be sure to articulate the virtues clearly before explaining how the critic should use them to evaluate a text. No length requirement.

15

Less and Less That I Can Share

Near the end of *An Experiment in Criticism*, Lewis said, "Those of us who have been true readers all our life seldom fully realize the enormous extension of our being which we owe to authors."[1] The boundaries of Lewis's being extended without apparent end, owed to Western authors of all genres and periods. At Oxford, Lewis showed himself to be that rare literary mind able to cipher one book's deficiencies and another's virtues, a burgeoning writer whose range of insight went from caustic comparison:

> Chaucer was very like Dickens—a virtuous, bourgeois story teller fond of highly moral vulgarity & indecency for its own sake, incapable of appreciating romance.[2]

to eased endorsements:

> I am writing a good deal and also reading. Before we left Oxford I read [George Eliot's] *Romola*. Certainly there is great comfort in these old-fashioned historical novels with a slow but languid movement and plenty of work in them.[3]

Over the span of Lewis's correspondence, we see a creative coming of age. His writing became more ambitious as he continued to explore new themes and rework old ideas through new poetry. His reading increasingly fed his writing. Long before he converted to Christianity, voracious reader

1. Lewis, *An Experiment in Criticism*, 140.
2. Hooper, *Collected Letters* 1.442.
3. Ibid., 478.

that he was, Lewis had a formidable knowledge of the Bible. And like any text Lewis read, he absorbed it into his writing.

> I have nearly finished the Venus poem and am full of ideas for another . . . a very curious legend about Helen, whom Simon Magus, a gnostic magician mentioned in Acts, found living as a very earthly person in Antioch. . . . I have written some of it, but of course I get hardly any time either for reading or writing.[4]

Lewis knew Scripture well even before he came to believe it. Simon Magus, the Sorcerer who sinfully sought to buy the gift of the Holy Spirit, was imaginative material for Lewis.[5] For the preconverted ambitious writer, such was the case with any biblical material. A character from Luke or line from a psalm made for the same straw as a scene from Homer or theme from Boehme. Scripture came to mind regularly in Lewis's letters. In a letter to Leo Baker, Lewis loosely quotes from the lamenting poet of Psalm 137:

> I have sat down by Babylonian streams
> And hanged my harp upon funeral trees—[6]

Lewis's increased appropriation of Scripture signaled further creative extension. Lewis was evolving as a thinker and writer. The 1920s roared with the discoveries of new interests and a return to old affections. On May 11, 1926, Lewis first met Oxford's Professor of Anglo-Saxon, a young scholar and writer named J. R. R. Tolkien. Not long after taking the post in 1925, Tolkien began the study of Old Icelandic literature. To help acculturate Oxford in Old Icelandic sagas, Tolkien started the Kolbitar (or "Coalbitter) Club. In this creative space Lewis and Tolkien began their historic friendship. Lewis recalled their first meeting in his diary:

> Tolkien managed to get the discussion round to the proposed English Prelim. I had a talk with him afterwards. He is a smooth, pale, fluent little chap—can't read Spenser because of the forms— thinks the language is the real thing in the school—thinks all literature is written for the amusement of men between thirty and forty—we ought to vote ourselves out of existence if we were honest—still the sound-changes and the gobbets are great fun for the dons. No harm in him: only needs a smack or so.[7]

4. Ibid., 447.
5. Acts 8:9–24.
6. Lewis glosses Psalm 137:1–2.
7. Lewis, *All My Road Before Me*, 392–93.

In the company of Tolkien and like-minded Kolbitars, Lewis ventured into Old Icelandic texts, reading the Younger Edda and the Volsung Saga, returning to him the delightful experience of reading these tales for the first time.[8] The Northernness that wooed Lewis as a teenager still called to him even after he was elected Fellow of Magdalen College, Oxford. While Lewis's tastes took him North, they also crossed the Atlantic. In a rather long letter to his brother Warnie, Lewis goes into a detailed assessment of Whitman, Hawthorne, whom he "admired beyond words," and James Russell Lowell, whose writing any man should be proud to have on his shelves.[9]

By the late 1920s, much of Lewis's reading was in the area of his professional interest. In a letter from 1928, Lewis complained to his brother,

> one of the misfortunes of my position is that my reading contains less and less that I can share with my non-professional friends. Except Pickwick (a very overrated work) I have read hardly anything this term which you would care to hear of. At present I am deep in medieval things.[10]

This intense, more specialized period of reading medieval texts plays a foundational place in Lewis's writing. It was from the depths of medieval things that Lewis drew ideas for one of his most insightful works of literary criticism, *The Allegory of Love: A Study of Medieval Tradition*, published in 1936.

Lewis's ever-extending creativity meant adding new authors to his imaginative storehouse, rather than leaving old ones out. Lewis is, we must remember, a man who read everything and remembered everything he read. We've seen George MacDonald's permanence in Lewis's literary thinking. MacDonald was an old author to whom Lewis's expansion as a writer remained tethered. Discussing MacDonald's influence on his *Dymer*, Lewis said,

> For we don't individually invent these things, perhaps. Look how the "empty castle" theme is present in *Phantastes, Wilfrid, & Dymer*. No doubt it passed into *Dymer* from *Phantastes*: but then, from it, in *Dymer*, I passed on to the mysterious bedfellow without any guidance from MacDonald—and only now find that he has got that bit of the story too, only in another book.[11]

8. Hooper, *Collected Letters* 1.701.

9. Ibid., 743.

10. Ibid., 754. "Pickwick" refers to Dickens's *The Pickwick Papers* (1837).

11. Ibid., 935.

Lewis describes the affect reading has on writing as the slow recovery of fragments of theme and meaning. Lewis asked Greeves if he ever had the feeling that in books there was

> something waiting there and slowly being recovered in fragments by different human minds according to their abilities, and partially spoiled in each writer by the admixture of their own mere individual invention?[12]

For the writer

Reading is a labor in maturation. The reader grows into new interests, gains a better understanding of old ones, and matures in her identity as a thinker. For the reader who has built literary relationships, this maturation includes growing in friendships with those who share the same readerly interests. Sometimes, growing as a reader means having fewer friends who can or care to understand the person you're becoming. One sign of maturity as a thinker and writer might be that you have fewer with which you can share that maturity.

How would you describe your intellectual growth? How has your change in taste affected your maturity as a reader? Have you found that intellectual development can actually lead to fewer friends? How can you continue to cultivate creativity, even if you find yourself feeling more alone?

Do try: Write a diary entry on how reading has changed you as a person and affected your maturity as a craftsman. Be impersonal, but be honest.

12. Ibid.

16

I Myself Always Index a Good Book

A writer acutely attuned to his craft, Lewis approached reading with an exemplary level of engagement. He culled books with a mind habitually honed for writing. In a letter from February 1932, Lewis commended Arthur Greeves for reading *Chroniques* by medieval French author and historian Jean Froissart. What's so interesting about this particular letter, and so relevant to Lewis's relationship with literature, is that Lewis lays out his approach to reading:

> To enjoy a book like that thoroughly I find I have to treat it as a sort of hobby and set about it seriously. I begin by making a map on one of the end leafs: then I put in a genealogical tree or two: finally I index at the end all the passages I have for any reason underlined. I often wonder—considering how people enjoy themselves developing photos or making scrap-books—why so few people make a hobby of their reading in this way. Many an otherwise dull book which I had to read have I enjoyed in this way, with a fine-nibbled pen in my hand: one is making something all the time and a book so read acquires the charm of a toy without losing that of a book.[1]

Lewis's approach is an example of engaged, systematic reading, especially fitting for an exhaustive tome like Froissart's history of the Hundred Years' War. First create visual annotations, advised Lewis. Make a map and genealogical tree to create a narrative of information in images. Then,

---

1. Hooper, *Collected Letters* 2.53.

create an index, a categorized way to list key ideas, names, dates, or any other information you underlined in a passage. Lewis believed that reading deserved this level of consideration. Indeed, it's a wonder that people give so much careful attention to other hobbies and so little to how they read. Reading had an allure for Lewis that no other hobby offered. He engaged a book through the intimate act of writing while reading. By conversing with the book through this level of active reading, he made the book his own, turning the dullest book into something with which he could converse.

Not all books called for this annotative method, and Lewis taught other reading approaches equally as engrossing. In 1945, after his reputation as a writer had been well-established, Lewis wrote to celebrated Australian poet Michael Thwaites,

> If you usually keep two books of widely different period and type going together (e.g. *Faerie Queene* & *Tom Jones*) you won't get bored. I myself always index a good book when I read it for the first time noting (a) Linguistic phenomena. (b) Good & bad passages. (c) Customs: meal times, social classes, what they read etc. (d) Moral ideas.[2]

Lewis's advice turns reading into an encompassing approach to literature. He advocates a system sensitive to the reader's experience and to the integrity of the book. Read books from different eras to stay entertained. Enter into the text with a system. Be attentive. Create an index that notes language anomalies, well and poorly written passages, cultural context, and the book's moral vision. Most important when reading, though, as we've seen Lewis also write in *An Experiment in Criticism*, is that the reader *receive* the work. "Your first job," Lewis wrote Thwaites,

> is simply the *reception* of all this work with your imagination & emotions. Each book is to be read for the purpose the author meant it to be read for: the story *as* a story, the joke *as* a joke.[3]

Lewis taught that the reader should accept the book with imaginative and emotional willingness, and in so doing, privilege the author's intentions. The reception of the work is the basis of reading. Once read on its own terms, the book is subject to fair criticism, and the reader in a position to give it. Lewis practiced what he preached. Every book he critiqued, he first *received* through close, engaged reading.

2. Ibid., 644.
3. Ibid.

It's well noted, and we've seen the evidence already, that Lewis maintained a certain degree of disdain for literature of his age. His handling of modern books reveals his critically receptive mind at play. And his critique of the twentieth-century novelist's work clues us in on what the *reception* of a book might look like. Commenting on Evelyn Waugh's *Brideshead Revisited*, Lewis said, "Waugh is a writer, certainly. Many descriptions, phrases, and long-tailed similes pleased me: but not the novel, as a novel."[4]

Lewis's issue was partly with Waugh's characters, particularly *Brideshead*'s distractible protagonist, Charles Ryder. Lewis faulted Waugh for not providing a balance between narrator and character. To Lewis, if the novelist writes a cast of sane characters, then he is allowed to make the narrator a "monstrosity," but if the writer creates unstable characters, then the narrator must be competent. Resolute in his opinions once he formed them, Lewis didn't let up on Waugh's *Brideshead*. The novel comes up again in a letter to Phyllis Elinor Sandeman, author of *Treasure on Earth: A Country House Christmas*, "I have read *Treasure on Earth* and I don't believe you have any notion how good it is. You have done a most difficult thing: the only parallel (for I won't admit that odious work *Brideshead Revisited*) is Lubbock's *Earlham*."[5] His praise for Sandeman shows that Lewis did receive some modern authors more warmly than he did Waugh.

Lewis was quick to praise his contemporaries, if—and this was quite a crucial *if*—he found their books enjoyable and well-written. In contrast to an unfavorable review of Waugh's *Brideshead*, Lewis described Graham Greene's *The Power and the Glory*—published the same year as Lewis's breakout *The Problem of* Pain—as a "most moving and enjoyable book," going on to say that Greene, "loves and understands his most repulsive characters . . . better than Waugh does his favourites."[6]

Lewis thought that Greene achieved a vicarious experience for the reader, while Waugh asked the reader to believe beyond reason:

> In Waugh's book the supposedly good end of the old rake had simply to be taken on trust: but one lives through the whole

---

4. Hooper, *Collected Letters* 3.97.

5. Ibid., 261. The Honorable Phyllis Ellinor Sandeman's *Treasure on Earth: A Country House Christmas*, an account of her childhood at the English estate Lyme Park, was published in 1952. Percy Lubbock's 1922 novel, *Earlham*, recounted his childhood at the English mansion, Earlham Hall.

6. Ibid., 180.

experience of Greene's haunted priest, filled from the first with interest, soon with compassion, and finally with love.[7]

Greene was one of the few modern novelists able to elicit Lewis's appreciation. Lewis, weaned on books that evoked the "dark abyss of time" and trained in Medieval and Renaissance literature, privileged old books over the innovative abstract forms of modernist literature. Modern poetry, with its *vers libre*, fared no better than prose. In June of 1952, Lewis responded to a correspondent who wrote to ask Lewis's opinion of a few modernist poems: "The truth is, these poems don't work—with me: they might with other readers, and, I dare say, better readers than I."[8]

A reason these poems didn't work with Lewis was their inflated style and ecstatic voice.

> The poetic species to which they belong—which might be called the Rhapsodical—is one to which I am very insensitive: I can't bear Walt Whitman. My feeling is that the more vast and supersensible a poem's subject is, the more it needs to be fixed, founded, incarnated in regular metre and concrete images.[9]

Lewis believed in making the abstract concrete. To Lewis, a work's form, its *poiema* Lewis says in *An Experiment in Criticism*, must control its *logos*, its content. But modern literature moved toward fragmentation in both form and thought. Not only did modern literature fracture theme from form, but some modernist authors tended to overreach for the obscure. Whitman's poetry, written in a voice of disembodied ego for which Lewis had little patience, epitomized the kind of impenetrably esoteric writing Lewis took aim at. Lewis's imagination wasn't the only thing baptized. It seems his criticism underwent sanctification, as well—"I can't tell you how I wish I could write something more encouraging: but between Christians the truth must be spoken."[10]

As sharp a critic as he could be, Lewis took much more pleasure in praising a book than he did eviscerating it. Reading good writing rekindled in Lewis the excitement that defined his youth, in the days when he and Greeves swapped letters about what book last thrilled them. He thoroughly delighted in a good read and wasn't shy about gushing over a new book. To

7. Ibid., 180.
8. Ibid., 202.
9. Ibid., 202–3.
10. Ibid., 203.

Douglas Edison Harding, English philosopher and author of *The Hierarchy of Heaven and Earth: A New Diagram of Man in the Universe*—for which Lewis would pen the preface—he wrote,

> Hang it all, you've made me drunk, roaring drunk as I haven't been on a book (I mean, a book of doctrine: imaginative works are another matter) since I first read Bergson during World War I.[11]

The Bergson Lewis mentions here is French philosopher Henri Bergson, author of influential works like *Time and Free Will* and *Creative Evolution*, both of which Lewis had read. Bergson meant a great deal to Lewis's gradual ascent to the Christian faith. He found in Bergson a "refutation of the old haunting idea . . . that the universe 'might not have existed.' In other words one Divine attribute, that of necessary existence, rose above my horizon."[12] So it's no small thing to compare Harding's work to Bergson's. "Who or what are you? Have you lived 40 years without my hearing of you before?" Lewis proclaimed to Harding.[13] Lewis went as far as to compare Harding's work as a "mix up of Pindar, Dante, & Patmore."[14] While Lewis claimed that much of Harding's book was beyond him, the "sensation" of reading *The Hierarchy of Heaven and Earth* seemed to Lewis like meeting a literary genius.

For the writer

Good reading requires attentiveness. A mindful reader knows that books are meant to be excavated. This means annotating, mapping, illustrating, indexing, reading with a pen in hand. The way to receive the text is to force the text to receive you. Enter into the book with an investigative mind. Converse with the content. Chronicle what you find.

On a practical level, how actively do you read? What could you do to create a system for reading? What value lies in indexing, cataloguing, or reading with a pen in hand?

Do try: Create a reading system. Be detailed. Create steps. Write out what each steps entails, what the reader should look for in the text, and make

11. Ibid., 99.

12. Lewis, *Surprised by Joy*, 204–5.

13. Hooper, *Collected Letters* 3.99.

14. Ibid., 100.

sure there is a clear sequential and logical order that arranges the steps together. Try to include at least three steps.

17

We Demand Windows

Reading sowed seeds in Lewis's already arable, creative mind. Plots, characters, ideas, quotes, scenes, and names all burrowed in Lewis's memory, often showing up again in his works years after he first encountered them. *The Lion, the Witch and the Wardrobe* is just one example. When Narnia fan Carol Jenkins wrote Lewis to ask where he came up with the name Aslan, Lewis replied, "I found the name in the notes to Lane's *Arabian Nights*: it is the Turkish for Lion."[1]

In 1952, Margaret Sackville Hamilton wrote Lewis about the chapter "Time and Beyond Time" in *Beyond Personality*, eventually published in *Mere Christianity*. The question pertained to how Lewis came about his view of time, particularly the concept of ever-present time, the idea that all moments are present for God. Naturally, Lewis replied by referring to the books that influenced his belief:

> The ancient books which put this view best are Plato's *Timaeus* and Boethuis' *Consolation of Philosophy*. . . . Modern statements will be found in Kant's *Critique of Pure Reason* . . . and in Von Hügel's *Eternal Life*.[2]

Lewis's idea that God experiences all moments in an ever-present state of time is a literacy composite, a thought made up of a range of books, including scriptural—"The nearest we get to scriptural support is II. Peter

1. Hooper, *Collected Letters* 3.160; "I pronounce it Ass-lan myself. And of course I meant the Lion of Judah."

2. Ibid., 228.

8–9."[3] When considering what made Lewis such an effective communicator, capable of such beautiful, clearly written sentences, Lewis's reading life really cannot be overemphasized. When friend and biographer Roger Lancelyn Green wrote to praise Lewis for his 1938 science fiction *Out of the Silent Planet*—the first installment in his Ransom trilogy—Lewis revealed in reply what reading led to his writing the novel:

> What immediately spurred me to write was Olaf Stapledon's *Last and First Men* (Penguin Libr.) and an essay in J. B. S. Haldane's *Possible Words* both of wh[ich] seemed to take the idea of such travel seriously and to have the desperately immoral outlook wh[ich] I try to pillory in Weston.[4]

Stapledon's *Last and First Men* was a landmark work of the imagination that influenced writers like Arthur C. Clarke and Bertrand Russell. And Haldane, atheist and evolutionary biologist, perpetuated the kind of godless materialism Lewis envisioned in creating Weston, the novel's malevolent, arrogant antagonist. Lewis went on to tell Greene that H. G. Wells was the best in the genre, and while heavily influenced by these authors, his own vision was to Christianize the science fiction genre:

> I like the whole interplanetary idea as a mythology and simply wished to conquer for my own (Christian) p[oin]t of view what has always hitherto been used by the opposite side.[5]

Reading was, for Lewis, a work of excavation. A book like *Out of the Silent Planet* serves as one anecdotal example—there are many others—of Lewis reading as a literary archaeologist. The ideas he unearthed reading Stapledon, Haldane, and Wells became the tropes he employed while writing his space novel. If there is a lesson to writers in this anecdote, it's that to read as Lewis read, with an explorative energy on which nothing found was lost, is to create a mind with close critical attention and cosmogonic imaginative scope: the writer's mind.

This was reading, for Lewis: the investigation, excavation, and reception of a book in all its textuality. Biographer Humphrey Carpenter recalls

3. Ibid., 228.

4. Hooper, *Collected Letters* 2.236–37; Lewis attributes much of his inspiration for *That Hideous Strength* (the last novel in the Ransom trilogy, published 1945) to David Lindsay's 1920 *Voyage to Arcturus*, which gave him the idea that science fiction could house spiritual experiences. Quoted in Green and Hooper, *C. S. Lewis*, 179.

5. Hooper, *Collected Letters* 2.237.

Lewis once saying to Arthur Greeves, "how one does want to read everything," adding that there was little in English literature he had not encountered.[6] We've seen how this might serve as Lewis's life motto, a thread that ran so true through his life. We can imagine the twenty-four-year-old Lewis reporting what the sixty-four-year-old said in a letter from November 7, 1963: "I reread *The Iliad*, the *Daisy Chain*, *Bleak House* and *In Memoriam*: a good balanced diet."[7]

Lewis read all he could, as many times as he could, as deeply as he could. He also read with an intimate devotion to the book's artistic identity. We see in Lewis a love for a book's uniqueness, its essentially individual quality, the particular kind of artistic reality each book brings.

> It's more that for me a novel, or any work of art, is primarily a
> *Thing*, an Object, enjoyed for its colour, proportions, atmosphere,
> its flavor—Odyseey-ishness of the Odyssey or the Learishness of
> *K[ing] Lear*.[8]

When Lewis said in *An Experiment in Criticism*, "we demand windows," he spoke to our need for the distinctly different experiences each book brings. He meant that we demand an Odyseeyish window, a Learish window, a Tolkienian window, and literature provides these myriad opportunities to view the world through another's eyes. Reading brings us out of our limited life experiences and allows us the experiences of another. Reading cures our myopia by placing us in the panopticon's watchtower. "The true aim of literary studies is to lift the student out of his provincialism by making him 'the spectator.'"[9]

Lewis's relationship to writing lies here in his philosophy of reading. Each work Lewis wrote was an attempt to give the reader a new view of the world. To turn readers into witnesses of and participants in what was for Lewis a transcendent act.

For the writer

To discuss Lewis's relationship with reading and its role in shaping him as a writer is a bit like discussing one's relationship with oxygen and its role

---

6. Carpenter, *Inklings*, 8.

7. Hooper, *Collected Letters* 3.1478.

8. Ibid., 102.

9. Lewis, "Is English Doomed?" 29.

in helping form breath. Nothing so inspired or controlled his writing as his reading; and of course, no part of Lewis's life so grew from reading as his writing. The many lessons from his reading life can be stated simply in three ways: *Read everything. Read receptively. Repeat.*

What books have created "windows" for you? What about those particular books opened up new views of life, the human condition, the imagination, creativity, or God?

Do try: Spend five minutes free writing about the way a book changed the way you saw the world.

Longing for a Form

I have let my pen run away with me on so congenial a subject & must try & get back to daily life.

LEWIS TO ARTHUR GREEVES, 1914

It doesn't matter what we write (at least this is my view) at our age, so long as we write continually as well as we can. I feel that every time I write a page either of prose or of verse, with real effort, even if it's thrown into the fire next minute, I am so much further on.

TO GREEVES, 1916

I don't know what I mean till I see what I've said.

LEWIS

From the age of sixteen onwards I had one single ambition, from which I never wavered, in the prosecution of which I spent every ounce I could, on wh[ich] I really & deliberately staked my whole contentment: and I recognize myself as having unmistakably failed in it.

TO GREEVES, 1930

Lewis's reading life was a long inspirative inhale, and writing, his creative exhale. Lewis was a writer's writer—lest we think that Lewis was given to mere bookishness—whose tireless reading proved more than an end in itself. Lewis received and then reified most all of what he read. We find authors like Malory, Morris, and MacDonald in Lewis's writing not just because he read them, but because by reading them they became the material of his imagination. We've seen how Lewis's reading shaped his creativity. How he drew his themes from his favorite authors. How the ways his sensitivity to an author's style might have helped shape his own. How perhaps the greatest lesson Lewis gives on writing, his very best piece of advice, is his love for reading. How all good writers are first good readers.

When I set out to write this book, I had three questions in mind. First, what sorts of influences, sources of inspiration, and catalysts for creative growth made Lewis the writer he was? Second, what specific advice did Lewis give on writing, a question to which the last five chapters are devoted. And third, I wanted to know the biography of Lewis's craft—when he started writing, what he wrote, at what times in life, and how he wrote—the specifics of his creative processes: all these details fascinated me. To see a writing life unfold as Lewis's so marvelously does—in all its creative cadences, collaborations, discouraging false starts, rejections, moments of inspiration, and successes—only deepens the authority of his advice on the writing act. To carry on with Lewis's writing advice, we should feel the weight of his creative life.

18

More with a Castle in a Story

Any look at Lewis's approach to writing is a study of intermingling modes, methods, and muses. Like all writers, some of Lewis's works are creative expressions of memory (*Surprised by Joy*) or contingently attached to a historical circumstance (the BBC's original invitation of what would become *Mere Christianity*). Others are tied to founts of creative inspiration: something read (Lewis's reading *Pilgrim's Progress* and writing his *Pilgrim's Regress* in kind), something envisioned (the "it all began with a picture" beginnings of *The Lion, the Witch and the Wardrobe*). And still much of Lewis's writing is an intellectual outworking of an issue, whether theological (*The Problem of Pain*), cultural ("The Abolition of Man"), or literary (*An Experiment in Criticism*)—and sometimes works with strands of all three (*The Great Divorce* and *The Four Loves*). But like his profuse reading life, Lewis's robustly diverse body of writing began in Jack's simple attic office space.

We have to remember when discussing a writer as associated with his faith as is Lewis that though the lion's share of his work came afterward, the writer's spirit did not suddenly descend upon Lewis at his conversion to Christianity. We might be tempted to forget that even Lewis's most famous post-conversion works come after years of a laborious love for writing stretching back into his childhood. The kind of formation a great writer undergoes from years of deliberate practice at his craft should result in more than mere analysis of the writer's work. There is richness in a writer's making beyond the books he writes.

Such is the case with Lewis, whose best-known books, *Mere Christianity* and *The Lion, the Witch and the Wardrobe*, and his critically acclaimed yet less widely read works like *Till We Have Faces*, were products of decades of practiced writing. By the time Lewis crossed over into the high green countries of Christian belief in 1931, he had been writing stories, letters, and poetry for twenty-five years.

From an early age, Lewis possessed the desire, persistence, and creative capacity that would mark the rest of his writing life. His initial entrance into that life had more to do with clumsiness than it did with some sort of blossoming inspiration. Physical awkwardness caused by his one-jointed thumbs—quite the inconvenient manual misfortune for a young boy—actually first spurred Lewis to write. Both Lewis and older brother Warnie inherited the physical defect from their father, leaving Lewis with an "utter incapacity to make anything." He was left to spend his time at the one activity for which he had an aptitude: writing. Lewis recounts,

> I longed to make things, ships, houses, engines. Many sheets of cardboard and pairs of scissors I spoiled, only to turn from my hopeless failures in tears. As a last resource, as a *pis aller*, I was driven to write stories instead.[1]

Perhaps the same providence that brought Bunyan and MacDonald to Lewis worked through clumsy thumbs. So Lewis was quick at work making stories instead of ships. Oblivious to what sort of happiness awaited, Lewis began writing. The practice was wholly self-actualizing and an empowering alternative to more hands-on hobbies, as Lewis learned, "You can do more with a castle in a story than with the best cardboard castle that ever stood on a nursery table."[2]

A writer was born.

For the writer

For any writer, the reasons behind the decision to write are preciously important. Sadly, many writers forget the importance of their childhoods in forming their imaginations. Remembering childhood brings the writer back to the wellspring of creativity. Returning to the nursery's

1. Lewis, *Surprised by Joy*, 12.
2. Ibid.

castles—regardless if joy or pain lurk within—brings the writer into the space of the imagination.

What moments from your childhood have helped—or can help, as you begin/continue to reflect—to form you into a writer? Do you find your childhood as a rich source of imaginative material? Are there places of loss or joy from your childhood that you need to write from?

Do try: Write a mini-memoir on one important moment from your childhood. It can be a moment of pain or happiness, a memory with a sibling or parent, a lesson you learned, anything. Tell the story of that moment's power in your life. Address how it formed you as a thinker, feeler, and writer. No length requirement. Just write.

19

I Have to Do It for Myself

Lewis's childhood home, affectionately called "Little Lea," played an irreplaceably important role in his becoming a writer.[1] Longtime literary executor, editor, and Lewis scholar, Walter Hooper, testifies to Little Lea's importance in Lewis's creative development:

> [H]ad not Albert Lewis moved his family into "Little Lea" on the outskirts of Belfast on the 21st of April 1905 the present Little-Master of Boxen might never have been born.[2]

Little Lea's literary presence, with its ubiquitous hoards of books and quiet corners, helped to habituate the novelist in training. Jack spent rainy days holed up in his attic study, reading and writing at his desk. There he wrote and illustrated stories with admitted "enormous satisfaction."[3] Among all the extraordinary aspects of Lewis's writing life, how early it began is especially remarkable. Lewis once gave Hooper an old notebook containing a story that predates *Boxen* called "To Mars and Back," which Lewis likely wrote around five or six years of age, along with another romantic tale of knightly mice and rabbits on a crusade to kill cats.[4] It was also at Little Lea that Lewis invented the worlds of Animal Land and *Boxen*, originally a

---

1. Lewis, *Surprised by Joy*, 10: "The New House is almost a major character in my story."

2. Hooper, "Introduction." *Boxen*, 7.

3. Lewis, *Surprised by Joy*, 13.

4. Lewis, "Preface," *On Stories*, x.

medieval play about "dressed animals" and "knights in armor," Lewis's first literary-topoi-turned-prose-tale about animals living modern bourgeoisie lives.[5] Lewis set to work on Animal Land with his brother Warnie, who—himself a young creative—spent quite a bit of time writing stories about a fictional India. And *Boxen*, Lewis's earliest major work of prose fiction, is the combination of Lewis's "Animal Land" and his brother's stories of India, a place lifted out of its real-world geography. Even the map of Animal Land had to be "geographically related to my brother's India," Lewis wrote.[6]

His imagination's early bent toward mice on crusade to kill cats shows Lewis's attraction to knightly heroism and dramatic themes. The first iterations of Animal Land, an antiquated play set in the "year 1327 of the reign of King Bunny," kept with these concerns. In a letter from September 1906 to his *Boxen* coauthor and brother, Warnie, Lewis, already equipped at seven years old with an instinct for character and a knack for dramatic conflict, demonstrates a remarkable ability to self-diagnose an incoherent plot:

> At present Boxen is *slightly* convulsed. The news has just reached her that King Bunny is a prisoner. The colonists (who are of course the war party) are in a bad way: they dare scarcely leave their houses because of the mobs. In Tararo the Prussians and Boxonians are at fearful odds against each other and the natives.[7]

It was in 1907, when Lewis, not yet nine years old, wrote Warnie about penning a history of his Animal Land. Already in Lewis's guileless imagination appeared the inchoate talent for world-making:

> Now that I have finished the play I am thinking of writing a History of Mouse-land and I have even gon so far as to make up some of it, this is what I have made up. Mouse—1 and had a very long stone-age during which time no great things tooke place it lasted from 55 BC to 1212 and the king Bublich I began to reign, he was not a good king but he fought gainest yellow land. Bub II his son fought indai about the lanters set, died 1377 king Bunny came next.[8]

---

5. Ibid., 14.

6. Ibid.

7. Hooper, *Collected Letters 1*. 3.

8. Lewis, *Lewis Papers* 3:80. Misspellings original. For more information on Boxen's development, see Hooper's Preface, *Boxen*, 7–19.

Not only did Lewis display a remarkable prolificacy necessary for any writer to move from project to project—"now that I have finished the play I am thinking of writeing a History"—but he also had a nascent ability to think fictively. As Lewis continued to work on *Boxen*, he wrestled with the story's creative coherence, connecting *Boxen*'s modern world to the kinds of chivalrous animal crusades of Animal Land: "[T]his led me from romancing to historiography: I set about writing a full history of Animal-Land." "Though . . . ," Lewis added, "I never succeeded in bringing it down to modern times; centuries take a deal of filling when all the events have to come out of the historian's head."[9] Medieval, modern, and completely prosaic, though Animal Land featured the talking animals Lewis was so fond of, it lacked wonder. Lewis said of Animal Land, "there was no poetry, even no romance, in it."[10]

In *Boxen*, however, he made a world. He created maps of peopled lands: "somehow—but heaven knows how—I realized even then that a historian should adopt a critical attitude toward epic material. From history it was only a step to geography."[11] These characters inhabited this world with story and history and relationship. Lewis was beginning to know the power of literary creation. He also came to know the sequestered pleasures of the craft itself. Lewis lost himself in his writing, so much so that his relationship with his father suffered—"The most important of our activities was the endless drama of Animal-Land and India, and this of itself isolated us from him."[12]

While the time young Jack spent writing likely didn't help his already distant relationship with Albert, it did create a unique bond between him and Warnie. This composite kingdom of Lewis's quaint Animal Land and Warnie's beloved India kept the Lewis brothers quite busy:

> The Animal-Land which came into action in the holidays when my brother was at home was a modern Animal-Land; it had to have trains and steamships if it was to be a country shared with him.[13]

9. Lewis, *Surprised by Joy*, 13.

10. Ibid.

11. Ibid.

12. Ibid., 41.

13. Ibid., 13.

These writing sessions with Warnie proved vital for Lewis's start to the writing life. The time Lewis spent on *Boxen* instilled in him a love for narrative prose, to which he would return again and again with works like *The Pilgrim's Regress*, the novels of the *Ransom Trilogy*, and *Till We Have Faces*.

> In my daydreams I was training myself to be a fool; in mapping and chronicling Animal-Land I was training myself to be a novelist. Note well, a novelist; not a poet.[14]

What incited Lewis's initiation into novel writing was a desire to read the kinds of stories he couldn't get enough of. Writing the kinds of stories he wanted to read sparked and sustained Lewis's writing.

> My first stories were mostly about mice (influence of Beatrix Potter), but mice usually in armor killing gigantic cats (influence of fairy stories). That is, I wrote the books I should have liked to read if only I could have got them. That's always been my reason for writing. People won't write the books I want, so I have to do it for myself.[15]

For the writer

Lewis's entry into writing teaches us two things. 1) Writers thrive in the right creative space. Little Lea, with its book hoards, lulled Lewis into creative comfort and emboldened him to make literary worlds. It's important to situate yourself in spaces that promote inspiration and steady work. 2) Writers can find their feet by experimenting with genre. *Boxen* served as Lewis's first attempt at prose, drama, historiography, and the kind of fictive cartography required for believable world making. Lewis remembered well the value of his early attempts.

What genres have you attempted to write in, and what has each taught you about yourself as a writer and the writing craft?

Do try: In 300 words, write a one-act play. Once you're finished, write a 300-word short story using the same characters you created from the play. Finally, write a 300-word history of your characters' fictional world.

---

14. Ibid., 16.

15. Green and Hooper, *C. S. Lewis: A Biography*, 169.

20

To Those Early Little Essays in the Old Days

Even in youth, Lewis displayed creative dexterity. He began new books while still at work on others. As early as *Boxen*, Lewis was writing poetry. His first attempt was a poem written as early as 1907 called "The Old Grey Mare." Like the chivalrous mice of Animal Land, the poem is about knightly bravery. At the ripe old age of nine, Lewis also set out on a juvenilia memoir:

> My Life During the Exmas Holadys of 1907 by Jacks or Clive Lewis auther of "Building of the promaned" "Toyland" Living races of mouse-land which will be very good when it is finished.[1]

Lewis's brother Warnie emphasized the "when" in the *Lewis* Papers—his compilation of commentary on the Lewis family—referring to Lewis's tendency to start but not finish a work. Lewis's early tendency not to finish a project shows up again more later in life, when he would admit to abandoning more than a few books. We can see *My Life During the Exmas Holadys of 1907* as a non-fictional foreshadowing of Lewis's later work in the autobiographical—a genre in which Lewis would also publish *All the Road Before Me* and *Surprised by Joy*.

Warnie also preserved a fragment of a Medieval historical novel young Jack started on while Warnie was away at Malvern. The book was entitled *The Ajimywanian War*. Warnie described the fragment "as a specimen of

---

1. Lewis, *Lewis Papers* 3:82.

Clive's early literary bent."[2] The story reveals Lewis's predilection for narrative, his novelist leanings, and his still-developing imagination. The novel is quite dull, containing none of the animal characters or quaint charms of *Boxen*. Like *My Life During the Exmas Holadys*, Lewis never finished the work; Ajimywanian ends mid-word.

Beginning in 1911, Lewis started to produce a slew of stories and essays. His early talent was apparent. Extant essays like "Party Government" and "Richard Wagner"—whom Lewis believed was the greatest opera composer in history and whose *Ring of the Nibelung* gave to Lewis a sense of vast Northernness—reveal a writer able to get his arms around a subject with clarity and advanced vocabulary.[3] About an early essay of Lewis's called, "Are Athletes Better than Scholars?" biographer George Sayer said it "shows his development as a philologist, or even as a philosopher, for he devoted most of it to considering the meanings of the word *better*."[4] Lewis even wrote a portrait about a family that lived across the road from him at Little Lea, ending with a profile of the family's youngest child, a boy named Arthur Greeves:

> He is, after my brother, my oldest and most intimate friend. I know more of him than any historian has a right to know of his subject, and I therefore leave him to those [who] can discover his faults more properly and his virtues less partially than I.[5]

Like his reading life, quite a bit of Lewis's formation as a writer took place away from the rather unpleasant English boarding schools he attended.[6] It was at home, at Little Lea, that both his creative ability and writerly habit flourished. A couple of reasons, the first more obvious than the second, come to mind. First, as we've seen, there was Lewis's childhood of endless books. Lewis the writer emanated from Lewis the reader. Second, Lewis's creativity benefited from several ancillary resources and inspirations. From the endless hours writing the many letters that would hone his fluid conversational style to the almost eternal availability of domestic

2. Ibid., 162–64.

3. Ibid., 230–32; 233–35.

4. Sayer, *Jack*, 69.

5. Lewis, *Lewis Papers* 3:305.

6. Richard James's "Lewis's Early Schooling" details the phases of Lewis's childhood schooling, helpfully drawing connections between his later writings and time served at Wynyard, Campbell, Cherbourg, Malvern, and with W. T. Kirkpatrick. See *C. S. Lewis: Life, Works, and Legacy* 1.45–78.

quiet, Jack enjoyed as nurturing an early environment for which any young creative could hope. In Jack's case, a few nurturing influences came from unlikely places.

Writers are made by myriad means, some more surprising than others. While what started Lewis writing was his "extreme manual clumsiness" from a pair of uncooperative thumbs, his inventiveness was encouraged by a little-known influence,[7] his postman at Little Lea. In a letter from 1913 to his father, a fourteen-year-old Lewis mentions his postman, "Jordan," who abetted his adolescent essays. As unlikely as it is that a mailman would contribute to the making of one of the twentieth century's most influential writers, Lewis himself testifies to Jordan's importance in his life:

> Who knows but that I owe more to those early little essays in the old days than you or I imagine? For it is this uneducated postman that I owe the fact that I was acquainted with the theory of essay writing, in however crude a form, at an age when most boys hardly know the meaning of the word.[8]

By this time, Lewis, the former novelist-in-training and experimental inchoate essayist, committed himself to the poetic. His early teenage years were creatively prolific. There is a gap in Lewis's letter writing between May 5th, 1912 and January 6th, 1913, which Walter Hooper ascribes to Lewis's increased creative writing.[9] Lewis had an early and enviable ability to form philosophical ideas and articulate them through ambitious attempts. A fragment of a poem that begins,

> Descend to earth, descend, celestial Nine
> And chant the ancient legends of the Rhine . . .[10]

written by Lewis in summers between 1912 and 1913, when Lewis was no older than fifteen, grants a glimpse into Lewis's ability to write perceptive, serious literature. Lewis wrote "Descent to Earth" after reading Wagner's aforementioned *Ring of Nibelung*. And like much of Lewis's early work, the

---

7. Lewis, *Surprised by Joy*, 12.

8. Hooper, *Collected Letters* 1.27–28.

9. Ibid., 20.

10. Lewis, *Surprised by Joy*, 74. Any reader interested in Lewis's poetic life should grab a copy of Don King's inestimable work, *C. S. Lewis, Poet*. King's book covers Lewis's entire poetic career, illuminating the literary style, philosophical context, and the publication history of each of Lewis's many poems. Where my treatment of Lewis's poetic craft is a mile wide and only an inch deep, King's work has the kind of mile-wide and mile-deep focus needed for a study of Lewis's poetic career. See King, *C. S. Lewis, Poet*, 28–43.

narrative poem smacks of imitation, with Norse themes and what would have likely been a twelve-book structure in the Greek and Latin traditions. In the *Lewis Papers*, Warnie introduced the poem, which goes on for seventeen pages, by calling attention to its admirable quality:

> its absolute merit and its astonishing maturity make it such a remarkable production for a boy of between 14 and 15 that I offer no apology for its inclusion in extenso.[11]

High praise for a poem written by a young poet with little experience from which to draw. Warnie was careful to note that the only materials the young author could consult were a series of synopses of Wagnerian operas published in a monthly periodical of the gramophone trade called *The Sounewave*.

Lewis's first published poem was called "Quam Bene Saturno," meaning "how well they lived when Saturn (was king)." Written at the end of his time at Cherbourg House, "Malvern," where Lewis attended from 1911 to 1913, "Quam Bene Saturno" was published in the *Cherbourg School Magazine* in July 1913.[12] Lewis took the title from the Latin poet Tibullus's first book of poetry.[13] It's a poem steeped in the mythology and literary themes of ancient Rome. In it, Lewis celebrates the peaceful rule of the divine Saturn during the reign of the Titans, and he does so through a simple rhyme scheme. Lewis was an impressionable writer whose creative aim was often to imitate classical authors.

Whatever childhood desire to be a novelist remained, they began to decrease, while his affinity for poetry increased. In a 1914-letter to his father, Lewis reported on an assignment given by Smugy, Lewis's very likable headmaster at Malvern School. Lewis hoped to do well on the essay. The options were to write a "poem in imitation of Horace asking a friend to stay with you at the most beautiful spot you know," a "picture of a specified scene from Sophocles," or a "an original ghost story."[14] Of course, Lewis, already ambitious to be a famous poet, chose the first.

This was at least the second time Lewis imitated Horace, and he confessed a fear that Smugy might think him unoriginal. Almost four months before the 1914-letter, Lewis wrote his father and included a poem in

---

11. Lewis, *Lewis Papers* 3:321.

12. Lewis, *Lewis Papers* 4:51–52.

13. Tibullus 1.3.35.

14. Hooper, *Collected Letters* 1.49.

imitation of Horace called "'Carpe Diem' after Horace."[15] Though by this time Lewis had become proficient in varied poetic meters, he, like most writers, felt more comfortable with certain styles than others, like that of Tennyson's "Locksley Hall." Had Smugy charged Lewis with a lack of poetic ingenuity, he, also quite typical of a writer, waited ready to defend his metrical choice.[16]

Lewis's range and experience as a writer broadened under the tutelage of "Smewgy," as Lewis was apt to pronounce. Just months after the second Horace poem, Lewis wrote his father a letter containing a work imitating Ovid called "Ovid's 'Pars estis pauci,'" a poem of "metre copied from a chorus in Swinburne's 'Atalanta in Calydon.'"[17] Beyond Lewis's transparent tendency to borrow from other writers, Lewis's early works of poetic imitation show a certain creative boldness. Even when a young man, Lewis—a consummate contender in the ring of ideas, given to verbal sparring, and pointed written word—thought himself up to the task of writing in and building upon classical poetry.

For the writer

Writing often begins in imitation. It takes a long time for a writer to find her voice, her style, and the ideas she most wants to articulate. Imitation helps hone the writer's style by copying beautifully written sentences, well-structured paragraphs, and a clear voice. Writing is as much about the writer discovering who she is as it is about the actual writing. That process of discovery is a kind of initiation into the writing life. Often, imitation is the straightest road into initiation.

What favorite book, poem, or essay could you imitate to help improve your writing's mechanics, structure, and voice? What is it about your book of choice that you admire?

Do try: Take one chapter from one of your favorite books—how about a Lewis book?—or take one of your favorite poems or essays and write your own piece on any theme you choose in imitation of the book's style, structure, syntax, and tone. After you've read the book, poem, or essay, you

15. Ibid., 34–35.

16. Ibid., 49: "I shall point out that some people like Pope and Addison wrote all their poems in the same metre."

17. Ibid., 63.

can spend twenty minutes on this imitation exercise, or you can continue on it periodically until you're finished.

21

With Greeves and Loki

Just as he happily shared with others what he read, Lewis loved to share what he wrote, especially with his good friend Arthur Greeves. In fact, on many occasions and on many of Lewis's projects, Greeves acted as a kind of creative collaborator. And it's in his relationship with Greeves that we see Lewis's love for and improvement in the craft of writing produce new blooms. Between the two, Lewis was by far the more accomplished, but Greeves also shared a love for writing, which Lewis sincerely announced as "the greatest pleasure in life."[1]

Greeves, whom Lewis knew better than "any historian has a right to know of his subject," served as Lewis's favorite and most faithful writing mate.[2] Just what their writing relationship looked like changed over the years and usually because of whatever new book Lewis was writing. We've seen through their companionate love of literature how the epistolary relationship between Lewis and Greeves—whose lifeblood remained "What! You too? I thought that no one but myself"—grew through book-talk. Every letter from Lewis to Greeves reads like a literary show and tell. Each filled with Lewis's "doings, readings, thinkings" about the beauties of both read and written literature.[3]

It was to Greeves that Lewis sent pericopes of his first major writing endeavor, an epic poem called "Loki Bound." By the time Lewis started

---

1. Hooper, *Collected Letters* 1.216.
2. Lewis, *Lewis Papers* 4:305.
3. Hooper, *Collected Letters* 1.103.

on this piece, he had been experimenting with poetry for a few years. But "Loki Bound" was Lewis's most ambitious poetic endeavor in his still early development as a writer. Written in part before and some after Lewis began his time with tutor W. T. Kirkpatrick in 1914, "Loki Bound" is a dramatic long poem about the Norse gods Loki, Thor, and Odin, with the plot of a Norse tragedy in the style of classical Greek verse. Lewis was eager to share his newest work with Greeves, who at one time planned on corroborating to arrange music for the poem, and who responded to Lewis's friendly nudge to take the MS home with him.[4]

Biographer Humphrey Carpenter described "Loki Bound" as Lewis's attempt to capture the "appeal of Northern myth and his contempt for the Christian view of the universe."[5]

By the time Lewis wrote "Loki," he was anchored in atheism. A spiritually embattled teenage writer, Lewis's unbelief lurks behind the poem's mythic lines. It's fitting then that "Loki Bound" is a tragedy about divine sedition. Decrying Odin's creation as an act of cruelty, Loki opposes the creator god. Creation itself is themed as the manifestation of cruelty. Lewis would work under this spiritually antagonistic muse for years, writing the occasional verse on the misanthropic God.

"Loki Bound" reveals a lot about Lewis as a young writer, particularly his inclined ability to write in a creative tradition and his affinity for collaboration. Since reading Wagner's *Siegfried and the Twilight of the Gods*, which kindled his vision of engulfing Northernness, Lewis found in himself an intensifying desire for Norse myth. With "Loki Bound," we are privy to a glimpse of Lewis's common creative process. Like many writers, Lewis would often read a work, be inspired by that work, and then write in the tradition of that work's author. We should remember that Lewis wrote much of his long poem while under the inimitable W. T. Kirkpatrick's tutelage at Great Bookham, where a work of literature was taught in its tradition and where the old great books were given the tutee's full attention.

Lewis swam in the streams of literary tradition. "Loki" was one of the first instances, but certainly not the last, where Lewis would impregnate the mythic tradition with new narrative purpose. Most famously, he returned to mythology in 1956 with *Till We Have Faces*, the retold myth of Cupid and Psyche inspired by a chapter from the ancient writer Apuleius's *The Golden Ass*. Mythic characters like Loki, Thor, and Odin—like Cupid and

4. Ibid., 59.

5. Carpenter, *Inklings*, 7.

Psyche—made lively vessels for Lewis's imagination. In writing within the mythic tradition, in re-enlivening those divine voices, Lewis shouldered the ancient literary conventions of dramatic deities with immortal moralities. Lewis, in a whimsical moment, mentioned his working within the mythic tradition: "the materials being re-created by the genius of that incomparable poet."[6]

When Lewis toiled in the mythic, he wrote in both imitation and innovation of texts like *Poetic Edda* and writers like Wagner. Like so many writers who go through phases in literary taste, Lewis seemed to have been stuck in this mythic mode of inspiration during these early serious writing years. He would imagine what new work he would set his mind to after "Loki Bound," a work he never finished, though he struggled to move beyond the mythic in which he so ardently labored.[7] Though he had other reading and writing assignments to tend to, the teenage Lewis returned to mythology any chance he could. His asking for *Myths and Legends of the Celtic Race* as a Christmas present is only one example:

> I am going to ask for "Myths and legends of the Celtic Race" as part of my Xmas box from my father: so that, as soon as I put the finished touches to "Loki Bound," I can turn my attention to the composition of an Irish drama—or perhaps, this time, a narrative poem. The character of Maeve, the mythical warrior Queen of Ireland, will probably furnish me with a dignified & suggestive theme.[8]

Lewis's work on "Loki" also sketches a writer eager to collaborate. We've seen his penchant for conversing about literary ideas. Lewis's utter eagerness to share his writing is at times palpable. We can feel his excitement as he shares with his friend: "I cannot refrain from giving you a few of my ideas."[9]

Some of those ideas included Greeves's setting "Loki" to "soul-stirring music."[10] Lewis's creative vision carried a place for the dramatic, and he imagined what his poem might be if adapted as an opera: "The next great opportunity for 'atmospheric' music comes (Episode I) where the theme

---

6. Hooper, *Collected Letters* 1.249.

7. Only 819 lines of "Loki Bound" remain and can be found reproduced in the *Lewis Papers* 4:217–21.

8. Hooper, *Collected Letters* 1.81.

9. Ibid., 77.

10. Ibid.

of the 'spirit of madness' is introduced. *You* can well imagine what it ought to be like."[11] Lewis found himself so caught up in fantasizing about what the work could be that he interrupted himself to regain focus: "enough!, enough! I have let my pen run away with me on so congenial a subject & must try & get back to daily life."[12]

After he shared his ambitious ideas about "Loki Bound" with Arthur Greeves, Lewis described an average day of Bookham, which comprised of Irish soda-bread for breakfast, morning walks, the *Iliad*, open time for reading and writing, and an English Literature course mapped out by Kirkpatrick himself. Often at the end of such days, Lewis would don his PJs and retire to his room to read and write.[13]

Greeves responded favorably to "Loki Bound" with a letter dated just eight days later. Lewis responded as a writer conversing in full workshop of his writing, and we see in Lewis a lively poet with an editor's mind moving through the details of the text:

> Your idea of introducing a dance after the exit of Odin etc, is a very good one, altho' it will occasion some trifling alteration in the text . . . .[14]

Greeves' suggestion that something be added to important scenes in the text resonated with Lewis's writerly instincts:

> Indeed, when I was writing then, there were certain lines in the play which I felt would be greatly "helped out" by appropriate movements.[15]

Here we have Lewis under the teaching of Kirkpatrick and companionship of Greeves, a brilliant emerging thinker and writer whose motivation and imagination flourished within relationship.

For the writer

All writing exists in a heritage. Every work within a genre. If a writer will find what kind of writing best suits him, he might do well to experiment

11. Ibid., 78.

12. Ibid.

13. Ibid. Cf. Hooper, *Collected Letters* 1.145.

14. Ibid., 80.

15. Ibid.

with various literary traditions. Devoting time to write within a literary tradition, like Lewis tried with the mythic, makes for good craft practice. It brings the writer out of his creative comfort zone.

What literary traditions have most informed/formed you? Novel? Free verse poetry? Drama? Which are most attractive to you? Epic poetry? Myth? Realist fiction? Least favorite? Creative non-fiction essay? Journalism? Short story?

Do try: In 400–500 words, choose a literary work within a distinct genre and write a new work using themes, characters, literary devices, or forms from your chosen text.

22

Practice, Practice, Practice

Being in Bookham under Kirkpatrick's tutelage nurtured Lewis's scholarship and gave space to his creativity, but for Lewis, to write, there was still no place like home. He found no place more comfortable or conducive to work on his craft:

> there is one comfort which must inevitably be wanting anywhere except at home—namely, the ability to write whenever one wishes. For, though of course there is no formal obstacle, you will readily see that it is impossible to take out one's manuscript and start to work in another's house. And, when ideas come flowing upon me, so great is the desire of framing them into words, words into sentences, and sentences into metre, that the inability to do so, is no light affliction.[1]

All in all, the affliction at Bookham wasn't too great. Under Kirkpatrick, Lewis enjoyed his most prolific years to date, immersed in reading, beginning on new projects, excitedly sharing his work with Greeves. By the spring and summer of 1916, Lewis had finished a manuscript called "The Quest of Bleheris." Standing at sixty-four pages, the manuscript was Lewis's most ambitious work of creative writing yet and his first major return to prose since his time on *Boxen*. Lewis's imagination was still derivative, his mode of creativity still imitative. "Bleheris" is a quest story about a twenty-three-year-old hero enthralled and inspired to adventure by the stories he

---

1. Hooper, *Collected Letters* 1.89.

read. Lewis *was* fond of writing versions of himself into his stories—e.g., *The Pilgrim's Regress* and *The Great Divorce*.

Lewis sent "Bleheris" to his favorite, and at the time, only, audience, Arthur Greeves, and would lose himself in talking about it just as he did with previous writing—"Oh vanity! vanity! to think that I can waste all this time jawing about my own work."[2]

Lewis, equipped with a writer's self-doubt, could be quite critical of his own work, and he remained somewhat unhappy with aspects of the story. With "Bleheris," we see Lewis troubled with trifles like landing on a title he could live with: "However, as I wrote to you before, that title is only waiting until I can get another better one."[3] He would lament about how stagnate the plot was shaping up to be—". . . at the worst it can't be more boring than 'Bleheris' . . . ."[4] Yet he plowed ahead on the story, offering his writing up for criticism: "This brings you the next instalment of 'Bleheris'—criticise freely."[5]

Lewis's study of "Bleheris" marked a return to old ideas from his earlier writing and an introduction to new ones that would appear in later work. After Bleheris and his companions, a dwarf and a squire named Nut, set out on their quest, they meet three men, one whose name—those familiar with *The Magician's Nephew* will be interested to know—is Wan *Jadis*. Lewis recycled his ideas. He was also a long-term mental processor. Stories and characters stayed with him well after he invented or met them. In "Bleheris," Lewis returns to the knightly tropes he was so fond of in his earliest stories of mice on crusades against cats. The story also features a temple to Odin alongside a Christian cathedral, where pagan and believer, "being too thoroughly busy in their daily life to waste their strength in shadowy things," live in harmony.[6] The former novelist-in-training's return to prose carries with it traces of his knightly juvenilia and the northern mythos of his "Loki Bound."

While Lewis was writing Bleheris, Arthur Greeves was working on a continuation of Lewis Carroll's *Alice in Wonderland* called "Alice for short." Greeves expressed doubt that he'd ever finish the work. Now this seemingly

2. Ibid., 183–84.

3. Ibid., 183.

4. Ibid., 186.

5. Ibid., 188.

6. Lewis, *Lewis Papers* 5:106–30; Sayer, in *Jack*—perhaps my favorite biography of Lewis—quotes this same line from "Bleheris."

insignificant bit of writing, which ultimately came to nothing, introduces us to a very significant aspect of Lewis's profile as a writer: his encouraging nature. His relationship with Greeves brought out a kind of creative accountability in Lewis. "I cannot urge you too strongly to go on and write something, anything, but at any rate WRITE."[7]

In a particularly poignant appeal for transparency, Lewis asked Greeves to commit to artistic honesty, to tell the "absolute truth" about his work, without which there is no point in sharing. Lewis positively prodded Greeves to send his work, be it the Alice story or any other work:

> you talk about your shyness and won't send me the MS of "Alice," yet say that you are willing to read it to me—as if reading your own work aloud wasn't far more of an ordeal.[8]

Lewis further admonished,

> I hope that you are either going on with "Alice" or starting something else: you have plenty of imagination, and what you want is practice, practice, practice.[9]

Practice. Practice. Practice. This is precisely the kind of writer's fodder I had in mind when I set out on this book! Tear away a strip or two of Lewis's immense talent, and we find the quotidian backbone of his creativity. It's the writer's best-known secret. Deliberate practice serves as the best training for the writer. In what might be one of Lewis's most perceptive moments into the writer's psyche, he points out that any kind of writing should be primarily practiced to better the writer.

Lewis understood that the writer writes for writing's sake:

> It doesn't matter what we write (at least this is my view) at our age, so long as we write continually as well as we can. I feel that every time I write a page either of prose or of verse, with real effort, even if it's thrown into the fire next minute, I am so much further on.[10]

Writing isn't—or at least, shouldn't be—a mercenary endeavor, done only to land the writer a publication. On his Alice story, Greeves struggled with the "technical difficulties of composing." Lewis's suggestion? Write more. Keep at it. It's through the deliberate practice of writing that the

---

7. Hooper, *Collected Letters* 1.186.

8. Ibid., 193.

9. Ibid.

10. Ibid.

author can find relief from the craft's mechanical challenges. The persistent writer can, over time, "gradually get better and better by experience."[11] Writing is its own creative space, the place where the author, neophyte or advanced, can freely learn his craft, where he can experiment, make mistakes, improve, and "splash about."[12]

For the writer

Writing is the best way to become a better writer. And practice, practice, practice: the writer's mantra. Practice allows the writer to venture out beyond her ability and then return back to the craft more competent. Voice and style, syntax and rhythm, diction and structure, intuition and perseverance are all honed in the practice of writing. Practice—nothing is more important to the writer.

In the last seven days, how often have you practiced writing? How can you make room in your day for it? What does practice usually look like for you?

Do try: Practice writing today for 300 words or one hour, whichever comes first. The project doesn't matter. It could be something you've been working on or something you've been thinking of starting. If you can't think of anything, try writing a short story using these elements: an ancient book of spells, a quest, a giant who has forgotten how to talk, an enchanted place, filled with dangerous and wild creatures, called Limbo Forest, and a mysterious king.

11. Ibid.
12. Ibid.

23

Lewis Proposes an Edit

Lewis repeatedly encouraged Greeves to share his Alice story with him, and when Greeves responded by sending along a sample of his writing, Lewis was thrilled. Though he could be stingy with his compliments, and he was never one to flatter, at times, Lewis served as a wonderful encourager.

> You know that I never flatter my friends—in fact my faults are in the other direction: so you may accept as a truth how this first sample of your work has knocked me all of a heap[1]

Lewis praised Greeves's getting "straight into the middle" of his theme "without any such dull descriptions as open 'Bleheris.'"[2] Lewis also praises Greeves's descriptive writing—writing that shows, instead of tells. Greeves's whole description of a river, Lewis says, is the kind of writing that "carries you away from the world into a dim, summery dream in some landscape more lovely than reality."[3] Long after his childhood attempts at Animal Land and long before he set out on major works of prose, Lewis knew that vivid descriptive language hallmarks good writing. His later prose writing exemplified the evocatively descriptive. Here is one of Lewis's own description of a "landscape more lovely than reality":

> The cool smooth skin of the bright water was delicious to my feet and I walked on it for about an hour, making perhaps a couple

1. Hooper, *Collected Letters* 1.200.
2. Ibid.
3. Ibid.

of hundred yards. Then the going became difficult. The current grew swifter. Great flakes or islands of foam came swirling down towards me, bruising my shins like stones if I did not get out of their way. The surface became uneven, rounded itself into lovely hollows and elbows of water which distorted the appearance of the pebbles on the bottom and threw me off my balance, so that I had to scramble to shore. But as the banks hereabouts consisted of great flat stones, I continued my journey without much hurt to my feet. An immense yet lovely noise vibrated through the forest.[4]

In this passage from *The Great Divorce*, Lewis's descriptive writing concretizes the compliment he paid Greeves some thirty years earlier. A vivid scene. Concise sentences that forefront the material world. Clear, direct narrative voice that calls attention to the environment. For Lewis, good prose is graphic prose. What Lewis praised in Greeves's writing—writing that paints a world rather than merely tells of one—defines his own.

But Lewis wasn't all back pats and attaboys in his feedback. Along with offering Greeves uplifting praise for those parts of his writing that warranted it, Lewis, already a keen critic, didn't hesitate to offer criticism. And Lewis was an honest critic, often quick to point out a work's weaknesses before praising its strengths. In this same helpful letter in which Lewis praises Greeves's style, he goes on to share a theory about editing:

> I have always found that if you are in at all good form when you write, corrections made afterwards are usually for the worse. Certainly most of yours are not improvements.[5]

Lewis intimates that the writer can tinker too much. Overthink his prose and leave his first instincts. Greeves changed "that," a more "simple, natural, and dignified" alternative, to "which," a rather business-like word. Given his love for conversational prose, writing meant to please the ear, Lewis much preferred the natural sounding word. Lewis also was not fond of his friend's overuse of modifiers. Too many adverbs and adjectives!

Forty years later, in his 1956 letter to Jane Lancaster—the one where he lays out five points of writing advice—Lewis says that the writer should not use words too big for the subject. He questions why Greeves would use "extremely old" over the plain "very old."[6] Lewis also cautions against heavy alliteration—which "would be a bit daring even in verse, and I am sure can-

---

4. Lewis, *The Great Divorce*, 45.
5. Hooper, *Collected Letters* 1.200.
6. Ibid., 201.

not be allowed in prose"—in one of Greeves's sentences, "shook her silvery sheen." Risking seeming "meddlesome and impudent," Lewis offered helpful criticism along with all the invigorated urging he could muster:

> you MUST go on with this exquisite tale: you have it in you, and only laziness—yes, Sir, laziness—can keep you from doing something good, really good.[7]

With a candor fostered by close friendship, Lewis freely calls out in Greeves one of the writer's gravest flaws, laziness. Greeves's work fostered Lewis's development as a wordsmith, editor, and literary thinker, a writer's writer capable of devoting as much attention to another's writing as to his own. Lewis's process of becoming a writer underwent continuous crystallization in these moments of critique of and thought about craft. For Lewis, proposing an edit meant enhancing a craft.

For the writer

Writing is a vocation of invitation and challenge. It thrives on accountability. Writers need other writers to invite them deeper into the writer's life. And writers need other writers to challenge them to make better art. With writing, as in life, iron sharpens iron.

Who has kept you accountable in your writing? What did that accountability look like? What about now? Any creative accountability? If no one comes to mind, who could potentially serve as a writing partner or partners? Is there a local writing group you can join?

Do try: This prompt is more involved and active in nature. Take the initiative to find a writer partner (or partners). Exchange your work with them. When you give their work a look, take notes on what you recommend they edit. When you receive their edits, make sure you understand the reason for the recommendation before you change anything.

---

7. Ibid.

24

Bleheris is Dead

C. S. Lewis fans might not know that he had a habit of quitting. Throughout his entire writing life, he was prone to drop a project mid-process and begin another. In a letter to Greeves dated July 25, 1916, Lewis wrote about a mythological poem featuring Hylas, young servant to Greek demigod Hercules, "I am writing at present a rather lengthy (for me that is) poem about Hylas, which you shall see if it is a success . . . ."[1] Like everything he wrote during this time in life, Lewis had planned to send this poem to Greeves, if it turned out a success, but Lewis admitted that he might not finish it, "perhaps it will never be finished."[2]

Important, practical, and somewhat encouraging to other writers with the habit of non-finishing, Lewis's writing life included several works that could have been, but never were. Lewis, in the middle of encouraging Greeves to continue on a new work and to send his progress along, admits, "I can't preach in this respect now!"[3] Indeed he couldn't. A pattern of in-completion had developed. Before he was eighteen years old, Lewis had behind him a trail of unfinished poems, plays, and would-be collaborations:

> Loki & Dennis & Bleheris, all our operas, plays etc go one way; perhaps they are caught like Wan Jadis in the Grey Marish on the way to the country of the past![4]

1. Hooper, *Collected Letters* 1.221.

2. Ibid.

3. Ibid.

4. Wan Jadis is a character in Lewis's "Bleheris" who gets trapped in a swamp called

108

He had also, by that time, gained a mature writer's heart of wisdom. His failed endeavors had informed his process and shaped his self-understanding.

> For my part I am at present engaged in making huge plans both for prose and verse none of which I shall try. I begin to see that short, slight stories & poems are all I am fit for at present & that it would be better to write & finish one of such than to begin & leave twenty ambitious epic-poems of romances.[5]

We see a writer aware of his ambition. We see a writer honest about his current scope. We see a writer doing what the best writers do, follow along whatever path the process led him; self-aware enough to know when a project wasn't working and discerning enough to sense when certain life seasons would allow for certain types of writing. Not every day can hold an epic.

Lewis's growth as a writer and thinker was testified to by the one man with the authority to give it, tutor W. T. Kirkpatrick. "The Great Knock" wrote to Lewis's father Albert to laud Lewis's exceptional intellect.

> I ask you, what could I have done with Clive if he had not been gifted with literary taste and the moral virtue of perseverance? Now to whom is Clive indebted for his brains? Beyond all question to his father and mother. And I hold that he is equally indebted to them for those moral qualities . . . I mean fixity of purpose, determination of character, persevering energy.[6]

Kirkpatrick touches on a character quality in Lewis that would seem contradictory to his tendency to quit on a project. After all, "fixity of purpose," "determination of character," and "persevering energy" are qualities we'd ascribe to the writer who finishes what he starts, not to the writer who declared that Bleheris died on the creative vine:

> as to Bleheris, he is dead and I shan't trouble his grave. I will try and write something new soon—a short tale, I expect—but am rather taken up with verse at present.[7]

---

the Grey Marish.

5. Hooper, *Collected Letters* 1.228.

6. Lewis, *Lewis Papers* 5.165.

7. Ibid., 232. Bleheris is now in the Bodleian Library in Oxford.

Lewis hoped to turn from "Bleheris" to something new, maybe "a short tale," if he could find time between writing poetry—an early love to which Lewis would always return—and studying for exams.[8] Kirkpatrick's praise of Lewis points to a deeper determination in the young writer holding the secret to his creative success: though Lewis quit on the occasional project, he never quit on the craft. Giving up on a project can improve the writer's process—possibly teaching the writer the discernment necessary to continue on one work while dropping another, honing his instinct to cultivate his skill in one genre over others—if that process is an expression of a lifelong commitment to the act of writing. Though Lewis's process, at times, included putting down a poem or moving away from a story, the grand narrative arc of Lewis's writing life was perseverance. At the center of the constellation of reasons Lewis succeeded as a writer stands his commitment to the craft.

Kirkpatrick also confirmed what Albert—and any who met Lewis—knew: Clive was brilliant. Equipped with the resolve necessary to be a writer, Lewis also had an intellect to match his commitment. Lewis had the ability to ascend intellectually to any conversation, a quality certainly present in his writing, which met the challenge of any topic.

> As a dialectician, an intellectual disputant, I shall miss him, and he will have no successor. Clive can hold his own in any discussion, and the higher the range of the conversation, the more he feels himself at home.[9]

Brilliant and possessing the stubborn ability to bounce back from an unfinished story, Lewis returned to poetry after Bleheris's early death.

For the writer

The writing process can be messy. Writers often don't finish what they start. The good news is that this is completely natural, even necessary, to the creative process. It's the writer's job to birth his idea. Whether it lives a full life or not isn't always as essential as bringing into the world.

8. Ibid.
9. Ibid.

Have you started a book, play, poem, or essay that you haven't finished? If so, why didn't you? More importantly, how did your work on that piece help your process?

Do try: Spend thirty minutes thinking and writing about the personal value of any creative piece you didn't finish. Try to get at least 200 words of reflection down on how the death of that work brought life to your process.

25

If Only I Could Get My Book Accepted

Lewis's repeated returns to verse were due to his love for it, and, after joining a cadet battalion at Keble College in 1917, to keep his mind off military life. Not long after the death of "Bleheris," Lewis returned to a number of poems he had been working on since 1915. In fact, between 1915 and 1917, Lewis wrote fifty-two poems, copying them into an old Malvern College notebook and arranging them in chronological order by title. Lewis called the now-lost collection *The Metrical Meditations of a Cod.*[1] In the *Lewis Papers* Warnie said of *Meditations*,

> Of the poems included in the "Metrical Meditations," three are marked as having been written in Easter 1915. Of the three, one was subsequently published, and does not therefore concern

---

1. About the title, Warnie noted, "It is perhaps not irrelevant to explain here the Ulster word 'cod,' from which Clive formed for himself the diminutive 'Kodotta' which appears so frequently in his letters. Patterson in his Glossary defines cod as, (1) 'a silly troublesome fellow,' and (2) v. 'to humbug or quiz a person; to hoax; to idle about. "Quit your coddin."' It has however a third meaning, namely an expression of humorous and insincere self depreciation; an Ulsterman will say of himself, 'Am'nt I the quare oul' cod to be doin' so and so,' and it is in this latter sense that it is to be understood in this context." Three of these metrical mediation poems were written Easter 1915 (*Lewis Papers* 4:306–7). Lewis would add seven poems to his meditations under the date "Christmas 1915"; "Noon" would be published. The poem "Ballade of a Winter's Morning" reminiscences Lewis's time with childhood friend Arthur Greeves, according to Warnie (*Lewis Papers* 5:46).

us at the moment; of the remaining two we select the following specimen . . . .[2]

What's important about *Meditations* is the creative and professional positions it catches Lewis in: a burgeoning writer with the increased desire to publish. This was an important time for Lewis as a writer. The desire to publish had taken root. Though he had seen his work in print before, an essay here and a poem there, Lewis had not tried to publish any major work. The period between 1915 and 1917 also saw marked improvement in Lewis's capability as an author. Lewis was already a skilled poet when he started collecting the poems for *Meditations*, but his time under Kirkpatrick only enhanced his talents. Kirkpatrick required perfection in Lewis's poetic structure and meter. We've seen how "The Great Knock" took note of Jack's progress. As Kirkpatrick wrote to Albert Lewis, Clive was cut out for the literary life:

> The fact . . . is that while admirably adapted for excellence and in my opinion probably for distinction in literary studies, he is adapted for nothing else. You may make up your mind on that.[3]

The poems that comprised *Meditations* boast of Lewis's maturity as a craftsman and betray his growing aspirations to publish. In June of 1917, before starting his military responsibilities, Lewis shared his desire to secure a publisher with Greeves:

> I am in a strangely productive mood at present and spend my few moments of spare time in scribbling verse. When my 4 months course in the cadet battalion is at an end, I shall, supposing I get a commission allright, have a 4 weeks leave before joining my regiment. During it I propose to get together all the stuff I have perpetrated and see if any kind publisher would like it.[4]

Humourously, Lewis added,

> After that, if the fates decide to kill me at the front, I shall enjoy a 9 days immortality while friends who know nothing about poetry imagine that I must have been a genius—what usually happens in such cases.[5]

2. Lewis, *Lewis Papers* 4:306.

3. Ibid., 4:39.

4. Hooper, *They Stand Together*, 192.

5. Ibid.

Anticipating conscription and worried he might lose his notebook, Lewis entrusted Greeves with his collection, calling for it after he returned in 1918: "By the way, haven't you got a reddy-brown MS. book of mine containing 'Lulluby' and several other of my later poems."[6]

Over the last few months of 1917 and the first few of 1918, Lewis's worldview took on the darker themes of war and atheistic naturalism. Lewis takes hold of Tennyson's violent view of nature and Locke's agnosticism toward the metaphysical. Lewis had come to loathe the spiritual, and his *Meditations* eventually took a final unbelieving, yet remarkable, form in what Lewis called *Spirits in Bondage.*

Incredibly—and perhaps encouraging to writers who've experienced the same—Lewis's first publishing venture ended in failure. With high hopes, Lewis first sent *Spirits in Bondage* to Macmillan of London: "I looked upon acceptance by them as a goal almost beyond hope, and sent my MS. to them first."[7] Lewis received from Macmillan a response similar to the responses so many other writers have received from so many other publishers:

> Dear Sir, We duly received your manuscript entitled "Spirits in Prison: A cycle of lyrical poems," by Clive Staples, and regret to say that we do not see our way to undertake its publication. Some of the shorter nature poems seem to us to have no little charm, but we do not feel that the collection as a whole would be likely to appeal to any considerable public. We beg therefore to return the MS. with thanks. We are, yours faithfully, Macmillan and Co. Ltd.[8]

Slightly discouraged but highly resolved, Lewis wrote to Greeves, "I am determined not to lose heart until I have tried all the houses I can hear of."[9]

Highly determined yet increasingly drained, Lewis let the anxiety of being unpublished get to him:

> I feel very weak and tired these days and inclined to lose interest in anything that needs continued attention. If only I could get my book accepted it would give me tremendous fillip and take my mind off the future.[10]

6. Ibid.
7. Hooper, *Collected Letters* 1.392.
8. Ibid., 392.
9. Ibid.
10. Ibid., 393.

Publication would stimulate Lewis's success as a writer, and he hoped, provide a smidgen of security. Lewis would receive the boost he longed for in 1918, when publisher William Heinemann accepted *Spirits in Bondage* for publication. Lewis was overjoyed. Lewis proudly announced to his father, "This little success gives me a pleasure which is perhaps childish and yet akin to greater things."[11]

Just three days later, in a letter to Arthur Greeves, Lewis repeated the good news, noting, as he did to his father, that William Heinemann encouraged Lewis to reconsider including those pieces "which are not perhaps on a level with my best work."[12] Lewis sent five new poems for inclusion. In his letter to Greeves, Lewis fretted about the quality of the paper and confirmed the title, "Spirits in Prison," an allusion to Peter's words about Christ preaching to the spirits in prison from 1 Peter 3:19. The final title of Lewis's collection would be *Spirits in Bondage: A Cycle of Lyrics*, published under the pseudonym "Clive Hamilton" (a combination of his first name and his mother Flora's maiden name as well as his brother Warnie's middle name.)

Lewis's experience with Heinemann taught him quite a bit about the world of publishing—mainly that publishing poetry would not mean growing one's bank account, even if it does grow one's reputation, and that even the best poetry was not expected to sell more than the most mediocre fiction.[13] It seems that despite his thirty years of publishing, Lewis never felt totally comfortable with the business of it all: "I don't know much about publishers . . . ."[14]

The publication of *Spirits in Bondage* also introduced to Lewis the kind of fearful paranoia all too common to ambitious writers:

> I only wish I was busy "correcting my proof-sheets": I have heard nothing more from Heinnemann. . . . I have horrid fears sometimes that he may have changed his mind and be getting ready to return them . . . .[15]

Fear fostered frustration, as Lewis received no initial reviews of *Spirits in Bondage*. Lewis learned that Heinemann was a poor promoter, as the

11. Ibid., 396.
12. Ibid., 397.
13. Ibid., 415.
14. Ibid., 464.
15. Ibid., 406.

absence of *Spirits in Bondage* from *Time Supplement* indicated, prompting Lewis to lament ever agreeing to let Heinemann publish it:

> . . . Heinemann—on whom ten thousand maledictions. Every week nearly in the *Time Supplement* I see a new book of poems published by him, but never mine. I can't think why he took it at all at this rate.[16]

Fortunately, *Spirits in Bondage* did eventually win Lewis favor with the critics. In fact, some reviews were glowing. Writing a review for the publication, *The Bookman*, Francis Bickley said,

> Mr. Hamilton[17] is as positive as Pope. . . . One might search his book for an accent out of place or a false rhyme; I do not think one will be rewarded. He writes so well that he does not fear to challenge comparison with his greatest predecessors.[18]

Other positive reviews followed Bickley's, and while Lewis felt a sense of professional legitimacy, not all of his subsequent poems were met with Bickley's affirming reception. Lewis wrote of twice participating in poetry reading competitions, where he read one poem from *Spirits in Bondage*, called "Ad Astra" in the manuscript version and "Victory" in the printed book, and another separate poem. "Both," Lewis said to Greeves, "were complete failures—failed of the first prize, failed of the second, failed even of a mention."[19]

For the writer

At some point, writing is about three things: submission, rejection, and acceptance. Eventually, the writer should submit her work. This is a big step. It means believing in your ideas and ability to communicate them enough to allow others to make judgments. But a writer is one who sends her work out into the world. Once sent, the writer receives one of two responses: acceptance or rejection. It's vital to remember that neither necessarily confirm nor deny your call or ability as a writer. Writing is what makes a writer. But the experience of acceptance and rejection forge how the writer

---

16. Ibid., 440.
17. Lewis originally published under the pen name "Clive Hamilton."
18. Hooper, *Collected Letters* 1.457.
19. Ibid., 459.

deals with criticism, and therefore, how she will exist in a creative field. Acceptance and rejection reveal a lot about the writer's fears, dreams, and what motivations drive her writing.

How can criticism, or rejection, of your work form you as a writer? What about acceptance? How does acceptance shape your creativity? Which, acceptance or rejection, is more productive in maturing the writer?

Do try: Take a text that you've been working on and begin the process of polishing it up as if you were going to submit it for publication. It doesn't matter if it's a short story, poem, essay, or novel. If you don't currently have a text that you can start editing, then begin writing something with the goal of submission. Even if you have no ambitions to publish, begin to revise and rewrite your text until you think it's ready to be submitted.

26

There It Is By Itself and Done

Back in chapter 11, "A Great Reading Event," we saw how a breakthrough in Lewis's reading life coincided with a new period of creativity. It was Christmas 1918, and Lewis had been reading Shakespeare when he announced to Greeves that he was "doing a lot of writing again." Part of that writing included revising a prose work he started two years earlier in 1916 called *Dymer*, about the "story of a man who, on some mysterious bride, begets a monster: which monster, as soon as it has killed its father, becomes a god."[1] An example of writer's persistence—he did finish more works than not—Lewis returned to *Dymer* periodically from 1916 until 1926. *Dymer* proved a laborious process for Lewis. At the start of 1917, Lewis said to Greeves, to whom he regularly sent installments of the work, about the original poetic *Dymer*,

> I can see my way clear to the end of "Dymer" now and will let you have an instalment next Sunday: three more will finish him, and after that I shall expect something from you.[2]

With his usual expectation of reciprocity, Lewis prodded Greeves to send along his latest writing and hoped to do the same, now that *Dymer's* end was in sight—so he thought. Lewis continued to send bits of *Dymer*

1, Lewis, *Preface* to the 1950 ed., 3.
2, Hooper, *Collected Letters* 1.269.

to Greeves, looking forward to that day when he could say, "Well, there is a book written: long or short, good or bad, there it is by itself and done."[3]

Lewis spent much of his time on *Dymer* with "no success" and often felt discouraged.[4] He continued to revise, tweak, and struggle:

> I am afraid this instalment is a failure. I have made three attempts at it and am not at all satisfied. Both in prose & verse & my everyday work the thing I take most pains with are always the poorest.[5]

The prose version of *Dymer* has been lost, but the poetic rewrite from 1918 survived. Lewis wrote to Greeves about its themes, its ideas of "self-destruction, both of individuals & species."[6] As Lewis described it, "nature produces man only to conquer her,"[7] and new generations rise up and destroy the achievements of the last. Here, Lewis's atheism was on full display. Lewis whittled away on *Dymer*, rewriting it in the metre of Shakespeare's *Venus and Adonis*, playing with the idea of changing the titular character's name from "Dymer" to "Ask," taken from Norse mythology's fabled first two humans, "Ask & Embla."[8]

It wasn't unusual for Lewis to work on multiple projects at once—he had been doing that since *Boxen*—and while at work on *Dymer* he was also writing a "short blank verse scene between Tristram & King Mark & a poem on Ion," which, he announced, was "a failure so far."[9] Few associate the idea of failure with C. S. Lewis and his writing. Perhaps because we forget that writers, even Lewis, are harsh critics of their own work. Or that even the most prolific, talented writers work in processes marked by frustrations and failure.

By 1926, *Dymer* had found its long narrative poetic form. Lewis's work on it became more collaborative, even going beyond the friendly council of lifelong friend Arthur Greeves. Nelvill Coghill, literary scholar and renowned Chaucer translator, became a creative counselor for Lewis. Lewis asked Coghill to critique his writing and entrusted him with a typewritten copy of *Dymer*—"a thickish folder of typewritten cantos in rhyme-royal . . .

3. Ibid., 285.
4. Lewis, *Lewis Papers* 7.136.
5. Hooper, *Collected Letters* 1.289.
6. Ibid., 419.
7. Ibid.
8. Ibid.
9. Ibid.

and I read it with all the excitement natural in one who is first privileged to see new work by a new poet," Coghill wrote.[10] Coghill gladly obliged the request, providing Lewis with detailed feedback to which Lewis receptively responded, expressing concern over a few issues, one being how the intentionally slow progression of the poem's story might connect with the reader:

> Of course I know we are here up against the devil of a problem: how to present bores without being a bore, or second-rateness without being second rate: complicated by the fact that the reader must be made to share that stage with Dymer and feel the spell himself.[11]

Lewis leaned on Coghill during the final phases of Dymer's long evolution, throughout which Lewis playfully but not without earnest said, "At any rate he has done his best to kill me these three years!"[12]

Dymer was finally published in 1926. Though Lewis doubted how successful Dymer's sales would be, or if it would sell at all, he was heartened by its encouraging reviews. Critics called Lewis's long work of poetry a "remarkable achievement," praised it for its "inevitability of expression," celebrating its "profundity of metaphysic" translated through superb imagery and symbolism.[13]

For the writer

A writer's work evolves. A writer might return to a text repeatedly over a long period of time before settling on its final form. Good writers are able to take the long view with their work, able to endure the frustrations and breakthroughs, able to let the work take them where it will. Before the writer can say about his work, "there it is by itself and done," he has to endure a season of, "there it is, not yet itself and undone."

Creatively, what are the benefits of taking the long view—rather than rushing through a project—with your writing? How important is it to let the work take as long is it needs?

10. Ibid., 662–63. See fn. 15.

11. Ibid., 663–64.

12. Ibid., 664.

13. Ibid., 675. See fn. 37: Hugh Fausset, editor of the *Times Literary*. See also Fausset's review as noted in *Collected Letters* 1.679–70.

Do try: Committing to take the long view, begin on a text that you will return to for weeks, months—maybe even years. Commit to return to your work every week until it's finished. Don't worry about when you finish. You'll know when. Just allow the creative process to guide itself.

27

My Imagination Seems to Have Died

Lewis's *Meditations*, the unpublished 1916 prose version of *Dymer*, and *Spirits in Bondage*, published in 1919, comprised a creative crest for Lewis. Lewis kept an impressive pace, churning through poems, some ending in publication and others unpublished and unknown to most. "Medea," a poem close to a thousand lines long whose title was taken from the mythological wife of Jason of the Argonauts, is a good example of the latter. Lewis announced "Medea" to Greeves in the winter of 1917.

> At any rate I am sending you Dymer's next excursion, and have begun the poem. The subject is "The childhood of Medea," & it will leave off where the most poems about her begin—shortly after her meeting with Jason. It will describe her lonely, frightened childhood away in a castle with the terrible old king her father & how she is gradually made to learn magic against her will.[1]

The poem, which Lewis feared would be a dull work, deals in themes of relational tension between Medea—whom Lewis likened in personality to Emily Brontë—and her father the old king.[2] Lewis wrote Greeves again about "Medea" to announce its fate, one "fit for the fire!"[3] Lewis "consoled" himself by taking up another project, turning "Nimue"—the literary Lady of the Lake from the Arthur and Merlin stories Lewis so loved—from monologue into narrative, hoping the latter form would better suit.

1. Hooper, *Collected Letters* 1.277–78.
2. Ibid., 460.
3. Ibid., 465.

It appears in "stanzas" of my own invention and is rather indebted to "St. Agnes' Eve" with touches of Christabel and some references to contemporary politics—by way of showing how much better I could manage the country if they made me Prime Minister. Sounds promising, DON'T it? It relates the events of a single evening—Merlin coming back & catching Nimue at last. This is the first stanza, do you think it any good?[4]

The stanza that Lewis included in his letter to Greeves begins,

There was none stirring in the hall that night,
The dogs slept in the ashes, and the guard
Drowsily nodded in the warm fire-light,
Lulled by the rain and wearied of his ward,[5]

Debatably not a good poem, and certainly not one of Lewis's best, "Nimue" gives us a writer still trying to find himself. In his study of C. S. Lewis's poetic life, Don King notes that the *ababbccb* rhyme scheme Lewis employs was not wholly his invention, though he claims otherwise.[6] While we don't know the reason for Lewis's less than totally true claim of originality, we do know that "Nimue" gave him a hard time. As with "Medea," Lewis had doubts about the quality of the poem. But he labored away on it, writing in a succession of styles with remarkable ambition, trying, "rhymed monologue—rhymed dialogue—blank verse dialogue—long narrative in stanzas—short narrative in couplets—and I am at present at work on a blank verse narrative version."[7] His continual labor didn't instill confidence—"I hope I am not wasting my time: but there must be some good in a subject which drags me back to itself so often."[8]

That he would allow the craft to keep dragging him back speaks to Lewis's resilience and commitment to careful redaction. When it came to prose, Lewis had the tendency to work quickly—though no less carefully—but with poetry he took meticulous care. The largely unknown poem "Hippolytus"—which Lewis submitted to a publication called *Odds & Ends Magazine*—went through several painstaking iterations, from "Hippolytus"

---

4. Ibid., 466.
5. Ibid.
6. King, *C. S. Lewis, Poet*, 50.
7. Hooper, *Collected Letters* 1.483.
8. Ibid.

to "Wild Hunt" to "The King of Drum" until finally becoming "The Queen of Drum," which appeared in Lewis's *Narrative Poems*, published in 1969.[9]

Lewis shared stages of revision with fellow poetry lover and creative confidante Leo Baker:

> I have done revised versions of Nimue and The Wild Hunt: the latter, I hope, is improved beyond recognition. At least I have reached a state from which I usually augur well—that wherein one looks back on the first version (once pleasing enough) as impossible, and thanks the gods for having escaped it.[10]

Lewis included in his letter to Baker a revised "Wild Hunt" with the question, "Is this good, bad or indifferent?"[11]

Lewis's letters to Baker contain some of his most honest moments of frustration at, as well as his more profound insights into, writing. Lewis placed a great deal of faith in Baker's literary discernment and in his ability to write remarkable poetry. Lewis was also taken with Baker the man. Baker, who once told Lewis he could see and conjure ghosts, had an almost hypnotic effect on Lewis. Lewis even offered to become Baker's "amateur disciple in mysticism."[12] And in a 1920 letter, Lewis proposed a collaborative work with Baker, partly in response to an editor's refusal to publish some his individual poems: "I feel, as a matter of conscience that we should try to get the thing published, though I do not feel any great joy at the prospect."[13]

His poetic passion was at an apex in his early twenties. Lewis longed to write masterful verse in traditional forms, and he expressed strong distaste for modernism's fluid forms. He especially loathed Vorticism's *vers libre*. Vorticism—with its terse free style, abstraction, and themes of dynamism and the machine age—represented everything Lewis hated about modernist literature. Lewis wrote to his father to announce an anthology of "counterblast"—in response to the Vorticist's short-lived literary magazine called *BLAST*—poetry meant to dislodge Vorticism's "ruling literary fashion," what Lewis thought to be a nauseating indecency "arising from the 'sick of everything' mood."[14] Lewis, intent in compiling his anti-Vorticist anthology to be called *The Way's the Way*, hoped to persuade "the gilded youth that the

---

9. Ibid., 466–77. See fn. 92.
10. Ibid., 505.
11. Ibid., 506.
12. Ibid., 472.
13. Ibid.
14. Ibid., 492.

possibilities of metrical poetry on sane subjects are not yet quite exhausted because the Vorticists are suffering from satiety," though Lewis admitted that the anthology may end by proving just the opposite.[15] Lewis along with another four poets contributed to *The Way's the Way*. Lewis contributed six poems. Because of failed funding the anthology never got off the ground, and Lewis grew tired of his literary pugilist effort. On two occasions Lewis wrote to Baker, "Now, to get this damned anthology off my chest"[16] and "The Way's the way to bankruptcy."[17]

Heightened literary passions, failed literary ventures, and the occasionally vacuous imagination rounded out Lewis's writing life in the early 1920s. In a letter to Leo Baker, Lewis, overwhelmed with academic work, confessed,

> I have been absolutely incapable of writing a line for heaven knows how long: as I have to do two essays—one philosophical & one historical—every week and have also been writing a paper for the Martlets, this is perhaps not to be wondered at.[18]

Lewis's academic and college society papers left him no time for creative writing. These demands, to say nothing of his home life, conjured the same inner struggles and artistic angst that other writers so often bear. Lewis lamented what he described as his decaying imagination:

> I am more worried by what goes on inside me: my imagination seems to have died: where there used to be pictures that were bright, at least to me, there is now nothing but a repetition of the trivialities and worries of the outer life—I go round and round on the same subjects which are always those I least want to think about.[19]

For the writer

The writer can be a loathsome creature, and the writing life, creatively barren. Very often the great test of writing is simply giving life to the practice

15. Ibid.

16. Ibid., 507, 513.

17. Ibid., 507, 513.

18. Ibid., 507. The "Martlets" are one of the longest standing undergraduate societies at Oxford.

19. Ibid.

of writing, even after the imagination seems to have died, by persistent effort. The writer can't always wait for the Muse to speak. The great ideas of what writing should be, the great moments of inspiration so alluring to the writer, and the great moments of creative breakthrough are all gotten at by finding a subject good enough to keep dragging the writer back to it.

What do you think Lewis means when he says his imagination seems to have died? As a creative, have you experienced something similar? Explain.

Do try: Spend half an hour writing about discouragement, creative anemia, and the importance of persistence.

28

Pen to Paper

In matters personal and artistic, Arthur Greeves remained Lewis's closest friend. But it was in correspondence with Leo Baker that Jack delved into his deepest ideas about the writing life. Introspectively reflecting on his waning imagination caused Lewis to question if he might not be taking himself too seriously:

> After all, what is the object of writing to friends except that of talking oneself into a state of self importance and the belief that ones' own perversities are matter of universal sympathy.[1]

Baker's part in their correspondence included sharing his theory of poetry with Lewis, the most valuable part of which Lewis quotes, that "a poet who is only a poet is not the greatest poet."[2]

Lewis agreed with Baker that the writer cannot just be a writer, but must be active in the world, from which his material originates. Lewis wrestled with his own theory of poetry, coming to agree with Baker's, with the exception that Baker seemed to confuse poetry—which Lewis defined as "the art of utilizing the informal or irrational values of words to express that which can only be symbolized by their formal or conventional meanings"[3]—and the objects of poetry, that is the words and their real-life antecedents. For Lewis, these "values" meant chiefly sound, word associa-

---

1. Hooper, *Collected Letters* 1.507.
2. Ibid., 508.
3. Ibid.

tion, and "their 'group' sound or rhythms which are above and beyond their individual sounds."[4] A word group's sound necessitated the use of metre. So then, the real test of poetry was, "could this be said as well in prose?" And, according to Lewis, "if the answer is in the affirmative the poem is condemned."[5]

Lewis thought the most pressing issue in a philosophy of poetry was the function that poetry alone could achieve:

> What we want to find is—that which is proper to poetry alone: what is the method by which poetry and no other art performs the duties shared with all art?[6]

Lewis's ripening as a poet is even more impressive when we look at his prowess in academic prose. His ability to pen premium academic writing became apparent at Oxford, as evidenced in part by winning the Chancellor's Prize for an English essay. The now-lost paper, titled "Optimism," forced Lewis to live with "pen to paper."[7] Lewis confessed that "Optimism" gave him "as much trouble as anything," largely because of his aim to write an essay meant to be both literary and philosophical. His fear was that he missed his audience, that it was too literary for the metaphysicians and too metaphysical for the English dons.[8] Lewis, having seemingly matured in his attitude toward publishing, wrote reluctantly of his desire to publish "Optimism." The twenty-three-year-old writer wrote to his father, who advised Lewis to submit the essay for publication:

> I can only find three motives for publishing anything—fame, money or reputation, in the narrower sense that may help ones' career indirectly. I presume that in the present case the last of these three is the important one: and in this, I do not think that publication will be of any use.[9]

Less concerned with publishing this work of academic non-fiction than he was with his earlier works of poetry, Lewis admitted to his father that the essay's appearance in some periodical would "remind people that

---

4. Ibid.
5. Ibid., 509.
6. Ibid., 508.
7. Ibid., 515.
8. Ibid., 515, 535.
9. Ibid., 551.

I exist," but might give permanence through print to an idea he might later abandon.[10]

Suffering significant self-doubt, Lewis thought his essay would soon be forgotten, except perhaps by family and friends. Lewis was becoming a self-assaying writer, already reflective, and regretful of "one or two things" in *Spirits in Bondage* and in both the manner and style of "Optimism." With "Optimism," we see a wiser Lewis, able to hear the advice of his Oxford dons who warned him not to publish an essay with an idea that might become a book—especially "when wider reading and fresh thought have given the chance to make better use of any really original idea you have blundered on."[11]

The months and years that followed winning the Chancellor's Prize present a Lewis heeding the advice given him: reading even more widely, thinking more freshly, and allowing himself the chance to make good use of his ideas. Lewis's social circle widened in the 1920s, and his place in the world changed with his 1925 appointment to English Fellow of Magdalen College, Oxford, where he would tutor English Language and Literature for twenty-nine years.

While Lewis kept writing verse, he began to delve into some substantial prose works. In 1928, he began what would be *The Allegory of Love* (eventually published in 1936). Lewis spent considerable time planning before actually starting to write. Lewis's letter to his father explains something of this pre-writing stage:

> You will understand that in a thing of this sort the collection of the material is three quarters of the battle. Of course, like a child who wants to get to the painting before it has really finished drawing the outline, I have been itching to do some actual writing for a long time.[12]

He continued, expressing just how the writer's idealistic sentences suffer the weight of factual reality.

> you can imagine it as well as I—the most delightful sentences would come into one's head: and now half of them can't be used

---

10. Ibid., 549.

11. Ibid.

12. Ibid., 767.

because, knowing a little more about the subject, I find they aren't true. That's the worst of facts—they do cramp a fellow's style.[13]

Lewis's deepened immersion into prose in the late 1920s and early 1930s marks a slight change in his writing life, but his spiritual life underwent a seismic shift during this time. By the summer of 1930, thoughts of God and Christianity were sprouting in Lewis's fertile mind, as was a new work of romance. This was a time when Lewis was reading works like *The Practice of the Presence of God*, the Gospel of John, and things like an essay on death by friend and future fellow Inkling Owen Barfield. New ideas stirred within him. And that meant new inspiration to write.

In June of 1930, Lewis wrote to Greeves,

> I hope you will not be disagreeably surprised to find with this letter the first instalment of a new romance. I don't know how long I shall keep it up, but it occurred to me that I could fit in four pages most weeks and that if I preserved I should thus get quite a lot written. Please criticize freely as it goes on.[14]

We don't know what "romance" Lewis was referring to, nor do we have any of the installments he sent to Greeves. In another letter to Greeves, Lewis called the work "The Moving Image."[15] Again, we have no part of this work, but Lewis described it as having a "great deal of conversation" and taking on the form of Platonic dialogue in a fantastic setting. We also know that Lewis was busy on a "modern novel," which likely refers to a work his brother Warnie called the "Ulster Novel." It's possible that it was the "Ulster Novel" that Lewis sent Greeves, though not likely that "Moving Image" and the "Ulster Novel" were the same.[16] Upon reading a fragment of Lewis's modern novel in 1930, Warnie wrote in his diary that he "found it so good that I urged him to take it in hand again, and he did not at any rate turn down the suggestion."[17]

This unknown novel remained the subject of Lewis's correspondence with Greeves throughout the summer of 1930. In going back and forth with Greeves, explaining his method of writing and sending his old friend installments of the novel, Lewis revealed something of his approach to style—

13. Ibid., 767.

14. Ibid., 899–900.

15. Ibid., 909.

16. Lewis, *Lewis Papers* 9:291–300.

17. Lewis, *Brothers and Friends*, 64.

As regards your criticism, I was conscious of the fault you refer to while I was writing: specially in the sentence ending "anxiety for the future." It is not that I am trying to be complex, but a habit that sticks to my pen from years of writing on subjects that almost inevitably lure one into a rather unsimple style.[18]

Lewis goes on to admit his tendency to unsimplify his language, agreeing to work on it. Lewis wouldn't forget this "fault." An awareness of the habit of overcomplicating his writing lodged itself into Lewis's creative consciousness. Whatever novel Lewis was writing, we can bet it was innovative and unlike anything Lewis had ever attempted before—and perhaps since. Following Greeves's advice to simplify, Lewis went on to write,

I am glad you noticed it and will try to simplify: though I should say from the outset that the matters this story deals with *can't* beyond a certain point be put into the absolutely plain narrative style.[19]

Lewis would later advise others on this point, writing to correspondents like Joan Lancaster to "always try to use the language so as to make quite clear what you mean" and "always prefer the plain direct word to the long, vague one."

For the writer

In poetry and prose, Lewis put pen to paper in deliberate devotion to developing his writing. The writer has to move from piece to piece, even genre to genre, with a sense of obligation to the work. The writer's first commitment is to serve the work. Serving the work means thoughtfully, reflectively, analytically practicing the art of writing. The writer works to develop a philosophy of what writing does, gain a better understanding of her role as an artist, and sharpen a beautiful and clear style. Above all, serve the work.

What have you been learning about yourself as a writer? What aspects of your writing need improvement? What are some things you've recently learned about good writing?

18. Hooper, *Collected Letters* 1.900–901.

19. Ibid., 901.

Do try: Identify a fault in your writing—maybe, overlong sentences, heavy dependence on passive voice verbs, unnecessarily complex style, redundant or one-dimensional diction—and then, being deliberating mindful of improving on the issue, try get down at least 300 words on any topic of your choice. Just start with one area in your writing that needs refining and work to improve.

29

Sooner or Later You Will Have to Write

Lewis's spiritual transformation spelled deeper contemplation on the writer's role and purpose. Before his 1929 conversion to theism, his letters betrayed an egotistical Lewis, one sure of himself and of his exceptional intelligence. One of the chief traits of Lewis's pre-converted life was his pride. But by 1930, we find a new Lewis, one far more humble, far more reflective on what it means to be a successful writer, and far more sensitive to the motivations of the heart. Lewis shared these reflections with Greeves:

> As for the real motives for writing after one has "got over" the desire for acknowledgement:—in the first place, I found and find, that precisely at the moment when you have really put all that out of your mind and decided not to write again—or if you do, to do it with clear consciousness that you are only playing yourself— precisely then the ideas—which came so rarely in the days when you regarded yourself officially as an author—begin to bubble and simmer, and sooner or later you will *have* to write: and the question *why* won't really enter your mind.[1]

Getting over the desire for acknowledgement had been a real struggle for Lewis—we can think back to his angst over Macmillan's rejection of *Spirits in Bondage*—but he learned an essential artistic lesson. The writer is one who *must* write, regardless of others' judgments, acclaim, or criticism. And the writer must play himself, forfeiting the desire to be officially defined by "author." It's when, Lewis believed, the writer stops seeking

1. Hooper, *Collected Letters* 2.931–32.

reputation as one who communicates great ideas and starts loving the ideas for themselves that he can actually write. It's dying to the novelty of being a writer that frees one up to go and write. Lewis discovered this unlikely artistic version of "he who wants to gain his life will lose it" by writing for himself. Without the motivation of the public's praise, Lewis found the act of writing its own reward.

> I had no idea of publication & at first very little idea even of showing them to friends, I have found myself impelled to take infinitely more pains, less ready to be contented with the fairly good and more determined to reach the best attainable, than ever I was in the days when I never wrote without the ardent hope of successful publication.[2]

Moved by a new understanding of *why* a writer should right, Lewis grew convicted about what it meant to *be* a writer.

> I am sure that some are born to write as trees are born to bear leaves: for these, writing is a necessary mode of their own development. If the impulse to write survives the hope of success, then one is among these.[3]

A writer is one who writes because it's a necessary mode of their development as a person. Rather than embraced, the dreams of success should be survived. The writer should hope that desire for fame "was at best only pardonable vanity"[4] Lewis seems to have lived his conviction. The Lewis we meet in his letters and published work after 1930 is markedly more humble than the Lewis before. Perhaps it's no coincidence that Lewis's most prolific years come after 1930. It's as if by emptying himself of vain ambition he allowed himself to be filled with new inspiration.

We begin to see a new creative capacity in Lewis, working itself out in new book ideas or the occasional new poem. Channels of inspiration came from several fountainheads, yet none more abundant than books. Lewis wrote to Greeves in June of 1930 about two recent books he read, Charles Kingsley's *Water Babies* and Coventry Patmore's *Angel in the House*. The former Lewis thought a work of sub-imaginative fancy, but the latter stirred his creativity.

2. Ibid., 932.
3. Ibid.
4. Ibid.

For Lewis, who had been seriously taking up prose the past few years, *Angel in the House*—a long, "half philosophic, half religious" poem about the mystical ways that marriage reveals and opens a way to divine love—had both creative and spiritual meaning.[5] The poem was significant enough to Lewis that he wrote to both Greeves and Barfield about it. To the former, Lewis confessed that *Angel in the House*—with its "strict & even monotonous metre" and moments of sublime syntax—rekindled his love for poetry.[6] We remember how much of Lewis's early creative expression sprang from his love for poetry. In the same letter from the summer of 1930 to Barfield that he mentions Patmore, Lewis included a poem he would later publish anonymously and then publish again in *Letters to Malcolm: Chiefly on Prayer*:

> They tell me, Sir, that when I seem
> To be in talk with you,
> Since you make no replies, it is but dream
> —One talker aping two.
> And so it is, but not as they
> Interpret it. For I
> Seek in myself the things I thought to say,
> And lo, the wells are dry.
> Then seeing me empty, you forsake
> Your listening part, and through
> My dumb lips breathe and into utterance shake
> The thoughts I never knew
> Therefore you neither need reply
> Nor can; where we seem
> Two talking, thou art One forever, and I
> No dreamer, but the dream.[7]

More than merely rekindling his affections for poetry, it seems Patmore's poem spurred Lewis to action. Lewis also includes this poem in *Letters to Malcolm*, introducing it as follows:

> I've just found in an old note book a poem, with no author's name attached, which is rather relevant to something we were talking about a few weeks ago—I mean, the haunting fear that there

5. Ibid., 901.
6. Ibid.
7. Ibid., 904.

is no-one listening, and that what we call prayer is soliloquy: someone talking to himself.[8]

Poetry enabled Lewis to approach spiritual truth with a poignancy not quite expressible in prose. Patmore brought together the spiritual and creative strands that ran so strongly through Lewis. Of the spiritual themes in *Angel in the House*, Lewis wrote to Barfield of Patmore's "fanatical love of incarnation" and the poem's privileged theme of the "Lilithian desire to be admired."[9] Patmore's treatment of the Lilithian theme of selfish desire lodged itself into Lewis's inventive artistry.

Lilith, the mythical first wife of Adam in Hebrew tradition, became for Lewis a symbol of self-love. Lewis repeatedly returned to Lilith as a literary trope. In a letter to Greeves just a few days removed from his letter to Barfield, Lewis considered how imaginative people might mistake the idea of spiritual growth with actual spiritual growth. To make his point, he quotes from George MacDonald's novel, *Lilith*, a line spoken by Adam to Lilith:

> Unless you unclose your hand you will never die & therefore never wake. You may think you have died and even that you have risen again: but both will be a dream.[10]

In *That Hideous Strength*, comparing the biblical Eve with Adam's first mythical wife, Lewis uses Lilith to illustrate an egocentric truth behind her character:

> The beauty of the female is the root of joy to the female as well as to the male, and it is no accident that the goddess of Love is older and stronger than the god. To desire the desiring of her own beauty is the vanity of Lilith, but to desire the enjoying of her own beauty is the obedience of Eve, and to both it is in the lover that the beloved tastes her own delightfulness.[11]

And in *The Lion, the Witch and the Wardrobe*, Lewis works Lilith into the history of evil in Narnia, placing the mythical character at its center:

---

8. Letters, *Letters to Malcolm*, 67–68.

9. Ibid., 904.

10. MacDonald, *Lilith*, 302.

11. Lewis, *That Hideous Strength*, 62–63; Lewis discusses MacDonald's Lilith more fully in a later letter to Greeves: see, Hooper, *Collected Letters* 2.118–20.

"That's what I don't understand, Mr. Beaver," said Peter. "I mean isn't the Witch human?" "She'd like us to believe it," said Mr. Beaver, "and that's how she is trying to call herself Queen. But she's no Daughter of Eve. She comes from your father Adam's first wife, Lilith. She was one of the Jinn. On the other side she comes from the giants. No, there isn't a drop of real human blood in the Witch."[12]

Lilith was somewhat metonymic for the larger theological allure Lewis found in Patmore. It was in Patmore's writing that Lewis's affection for spiritual truth, tightly wound up with his love for poetry, deepened. Lewis wrote to Greeves in July, 1930,

> I don't remember for many years to have felt so disposed for new reading as I do now, and specially poetry. Everything seems—you know the feeling—to be beginning again and one has the sense of immortality.[13]

For the writer

Writing is more about heart than hands. For Lewis, the words on the page, the sentences' style, and the possible success of the book are secondarily important to identifying how the writer sees himself and what makes him write. Sooner and later, the art reveals the impulse. The impulse not only determines what kind of work the writer creates but also what kind of person the writer becomes.

Why do you write? What do you hope to gain by it? More importantly, must you write?

Do try: Write a brief personal memoir on why you write. Address what drives you. Excavate the passion that first caused you to write. Expound on what brings you back to the page and why you love the craft.

---

12. Lewis, *The Lion, the Witch and the Wardrobe*, 81.

13. Hooper, *Collected Letters 1*. 915.

30

Kill the Part of You That Wants Success

The idea of what constituted the writer's motivation remained important to Lewis. In looking at Lewis and writing, we do well to remember that much of Lewis's thinking on why the writer should write was tied to critiquing and providing feedback on writing. This aspect of Lewis's writing life can't be overstated. Lewis's criticism of others' writing served two purposes, to improve a work of literature at the level of craft and style and to speak into the writer's life. To both ends, Lewis gave considerable time and attention. But it's his commitment to the second purpose that imbues the first with the kind of weighty meaning that defined Lewis's relationship with others.

Lewis reveled in critiquing another's writing, not only because of his love of the well-written word, but also because he cared about the writer. These two concerns thread through Lewis's correspondence with writers, and are, perhaps, most apparent in his encouragement to a disheartened Greeves at a time of writing failure. In August, 1930, Lewis wrote,

> The first thing, when one is worried as to whether one will have to have an operation or whether one is a literary failure, is *to assume absolutely mercilessly that the worst is true*, and to ask *What Then?*[1]

Lewis goes on to say that if the worst turns out in the end to be false, and the writer is not an absolute literary failure, then so much the better.

---

1. Hooper, *Collected Letters* 1.924.

There's hope. But until that question is ultimately settled, the writer must dismiss the uncertainty of it altogether and persist as if he is, in fact, an absolute literary failure. So, what then?

To counsel Greeves, Lewis drew from personal experience and recalled Heinemann's rejection of *Dymer*:

> So as soon as I read your letter I bethought me of myself on the evening when the MS of *Dymer* came back from Heinemanns rejected without a word of criticism or encouragement: and I remembered that after a very miserable night I sat down to assume the worst, as I advise you to do, and *on that basis* to come to terms with the situation.[2]

With the sage wisdom of experience, Lewis dispels the notion that publication success dissolves the writing life's disappointments. Even Lewis's successes by the time he wrote this letter to Greeves in 1930 didn't satisfy the ambition that defined his life until that point.

> To you, no doubt, at the moment it seems that to read your own book in print and to have it liked by a few friends would be ample bliss, whether any one bought it or not. Believe me, Arthur, this is an *absolute delusion*. It might satisfy you for a moment: but very soon, if it didn't sell, you would find yourself just as disappointed as you are now. So that in this sense I am *still* as disappointed an author as you. From the age of sixteen onwards I had one single ambition, from which I never wavered, in the prosecution of which I spent every ounce I could, on wh[ich] I really & deliberately staked my whole contentment: and I recognize myself as having unmistakably failed in it.[3]

In what might be the most fascinating glimpse into Lewis's layered creative psyche, Lewis included in his letter to Greeves a document he wrote to himself after *Dymer*'s initial rejection in 1926 "to find out by the analysis of my present disappointment what exactly it is I hope to gain by poetical success."[4] In his self-addressed introspection, Lewis considered every possible reason for the severity of his dejection. He, in fact, lists thirteen major—as well as several minor—possible causes for his disappointment, ranging from a simple desire for personal fame to a desire for a great work of literature to proving to himself that he could call himself a

2. Ibid.
3. Ibid., 925.
4. Ibid., 928.

legitimate poet. Among his considerations of motive, Lewis comes close to a conclusion:

> My desire then contains two elements. (a) The desire for some proof to myself that I am a poet. (b) The desire that my poet-hood should be acknowledged even if no one knows that it is mine. (b) is a means to (a) but it is not valued only as a means.[5]

Both desires—that for self-verification and outside acknowledge-ment—are in essence, "manifestations of the single desire for what may be called mental or spiritual rank."[6] The craven desire to publish was a kind of "self love" from which Lewis needed to turn. The ambition that so natu-rally comes with the writing life proved to be a regression back into the "tumult of self-love" that characterized his preconverted work. Writing had changed for Lewis, now.

Writing, like reading, was meant to draw the person out of himself. Writing was meant to be done from an "interest in the object," not from the "privileged position of seer of the object."[7] Lewis concluded that: "The only healthy or happy or eternal life is to look so steadily on the World that the representation 'Me' fades away."[8]

Placing the writer's "me" at the center of his creative consciousness was, for Lewis, a "disease" of which he wanted Greeves to be cured. Held as an exercise in humility—a new conviction of Lewis, from which he even advises Greeves to "read what Bunyan says about the valley of humilia-tion"—writing treated the disease.[9] Lewis believed that unless the writer abandoned his selfish ambition he would fall into the same trap of dejec-tion again. And if Christianity had any say in the writer's motives, then the writer must expect God to remove any trait that didn't promote the selfless creed, "Thy Kingdom Come":

> The side of me which longs, not to write, for no one can stop us doing that, but to be approved as a writer, is not the side of us that is really worth much. And depend upon it, unless God has abandoned us, he will find means to cauterise that side somehow or other. If we can take the pain well and truly now and by it

5. Ibid., 930.
6. Ibid.
7. Ibid.
8. Ibid.
9. Ibid., 925.

forever get over the wish to be distinguished beyond our fellows, well: if not we shall get it again in some other form.[10]

Lewis believed that God had been especially kind to him and Greeves by granting them failure early in life. Living until the age of sixty before discovering that literary "success" was mere "dust and ashes" was a far worse fate than experiencing dejection early on. Dejection, in reality, brings a dependence on God unknown to those whose self-sustaining success moves them through their writing lives:

> one creeps home, tired and bruised, into a state of mind that is really restful, when all ones ambitions have been given up. Then one can really for the first time say "Thy Kingdom come": for in that Kingdom there will be no preeminences and a man must have reached the stage of not caring two straws about his own status before he can enter it.[11]

All of Greeves's disillusion, the sting of having his work rejected, makes for a necessary death into which Lewis implores Greeves to go further:

> I implore you, then, seriously, to regard your present trouble as an opportunity for carrying the dying process a stage further. . . . I "implore" because such disappointments, if *accepted* as death, and therefore the beginning of new life, are infinitely valuable: but if not, are terrible dangers.[12]

Instead of consoling Greeves with a word of literary encouragement, Lewis refrains for the sake of this death's "first step," beseeching Greeves, "whether you are going to be a writer or not, *in either case*, you must so far die as to get over putting that question first."[13]

The writer who refuses this spiritual lesson of death is doomed to repeat it. "Until we learn better," Lewis warned, "we shall get this kind of suffering again and again."[14] As his transparency in advising Greeves allows us to see, Lewis did suffer again and again as he approached the craft through years of shamelessly selfish desire.

10. Ibid., 926.
11. Ibid.
12. Ibid.
13. Ibid., 927.
14. Ibid.

I would have given almost *anything*—I shudder to think what I would have given if I had been allowed—to be a successful writer.[15]

In trying to spare Greeves from this writer's bane of vain ambition, to be the kind of writer who works for love of the craft and not from a mercenary spirit, Lewis admonishes—"kill the part of you that wants success."[16]

For the writer

Writing requires introspection. The writer must reckon his with work, and he must, more importantly, contend with himself if the work turns out a disappointment. Paradoxically, it isn't the successful endeavor or the award-winning work that most clearly allows an introspective look. It's often failure that forces the writer to reflect on why he has given himself to writing and why he will continue to. Success in writing, however that may be defined, doesn't always promote the right motives in the writer. And as unwelcomed as failure is, in it could lie lessons that will serve the writer well throughout his creative life.

What lessons have you learned from your creative failures? Or if you've yet to experience rejection or discouragement due to writing, think of any goal you failed to meet. Does Lewis's advice to Greeves about killing the part that wants success resonate with you? How?

Do try: Write about a time in life when you experienced failure in your writing or felt discouraged from not meeting an important goal. Your topic is what that disappointing time taught you about yourself as a person and writer. Make this a thesis-driven essay; that is, build your essay on one controlling idea.

15. Ibid.
16. Ibid.

31

The Perfect Circle is Made

Just ten days after Lewis's letter admonishing Greeves to kill his desire for success, Lewis followed up with what he contemplatively conceived of as a nobler and purer motive for writing. As previously discussed, Lewis encouraged Greeves to "play himself" when he writes, to avoid the pretension of officially regarding himself as an author, and to love the ideas, which will "begin to bubble and simmer" until the writer simply has to write.[1] This letter from August 28, 1930, is worth circling back to, as it contains Lewis's ascent into a thoroughly Christian philosophy of writing.

In his emergent philosophy, Lewis gave preeminence to the process, rather than the end goal, of writing. The writer should embrace the truth that his most successful might soon be forgotten while those pieces he considered failures "may survive and be read and be an influence when English is a dead language."[2]

Or maybe the true good of a book is its affect upon its author, certainly an even more important consideration as the craft concerns the writer's soul. This was the case with Ibsen's plays, of whom Lewis reminded Greeves: "every play he wrote had been written for the purgation of his own heart"—the true good of a book is its refinement of the author.[3] Lewis testifies to this dynamic of personal benefit in his life: "I feel quite certain

---

1. Hooper, *Collected Letters* 1.931–32.
2. Ibid., 931.
3. Ibid., 932.

that I could not have certain good things now if I had not gone through the writing of Dymer."[4]

Dymer, if for no other reason than its personal benefit to Lewis's maturity as a writer, had to be written. Who knows what works would not have come had Lewis never wrestled with *Dymer*'s many drafts. It's the process of writing that works in the writer to produce lasting growth. What matters most to Lewis, the truth he most wants Greeves to embrace, is that the writer see the creative process as essential to his existence, rather than merely beneficial to his success. It's worth recalling Lewis's words to Greeves on the necessary role writing should play in the writer's life:

> I am sure that some are born to write as trees are born to bear leaves: for these, writing is a necessary mode of their own development. If the impulse to write survives the hope of success, then one is among these.[5]

But if the writer's motives are driven by success, then the impulse to write is, at best, "pardonable vanity" and at worst an ephemeral inclination that will vanish once the hope for success does. To writers, the act of writing is a necessity. And as Lewis's enduring passion for the craft proved, only the writer's internal state can confirm his commitment or comb through his motives to write—"So that whether the necessity and duty of writing is laid on a man or not can soon be discovered by his own feelings."[6]

Lewis's counsel to Greeves takes him to ultimate dependence on God. The "ordinary rules of morality" should help guide why, and what, he writes. But for a work's end results, "for ultimate justifications & results," the writer should "trust to God."[7] In an analogy reminiscent of Jesus's words in the Gospel of Luke—"consider the lilies of the field"—Lewis encouraged Greeves to look at the unknowability of creation's results.[8]

> The bee builds its cell and the bird its nest, probably with no knowledge of what purpose they will serve: another sees to that. Nobody knows what the result of your writing, or mine . . . will be. But I think we may depend upon it that endless and devoted work on an object to which a man feels seriously impelled will tell

---

4. Ibid.

5. Ibid.

6. Ibid.

7. Ibid., 932–33.

8. Luke 12:27.

somewhere or other: himself or others, in this world or others, will reap a harvest exactly proportional to the output.[9]

If the writer, like the bee, need not worry about an outcome behind his control, then what is his purpose? To keep writing. Lewis, by this time surrendering to a selflessly Christian view of the craft, presented Greeves with an uplifting and responsible philosophy of writing. The writer's task is to receive God's revelatory beauty for the chief end of reflecting it back to Him.

> Beauty descends from God into nature: but there it would perish and does except when a Man appreciates it with worship and thus as it were *sends it back* to God: so that through his consciousness what descended ascends again and the perfect circle is made.[10]

For the writer

Writing is undeniably spiritual. It requires constant existential introspection, continual meditation on the world and human condition, and a certain measure of faith in the power and meaning of human language. Writing is also potentially narcissistic. The writer must look at her feelings and thoughts, must trust her judgments about the world, and must have incredible faith that *her* words hold power and meaning. What determines whether the writer's work will reach beyond the self-centered toward the spiritual is often her commitment to the process of writing and her peace with its outcome.

Spiritually and personally, how do you see the process of writing? What does it mean to your ego? What does it mean to your view of God? Upon self-reflection, do you write for the craft or the outcome?

Do try: Write on writing, specifically taking on the subject of how you think a writer should view his work and its outcome. Explore your thoughts on the meaning of the writing process. Keep in mind related issues, like what outcomes the writer should hope for.

9. Ibid., 932–33.
10. Ibid., 933.

32

Bad by Any Theory of Style

Lewis first accepted Christianity in the early morning hours of September 20, 1931. His decision was helped by the company and conversation of literary companions J. R. R. Tolkien and Hugo Dyson the night before, on September 19. Lewis had dinner with Tolkien and Dyson on the night of the 19th at Magdalen College and afterwards went on a late-night jaunt down Addison's Walk. The conversation turned to myth and why, on the one hand, Lewis enjoyed and was moved by "the idea of a god sacrificing himself" in pagan stories while, on the other, rather illogically being repelled by the Gospel accounts of Jesus. Tolkien and Dyson helped convince Lewis that the Christ myth is superior to its pagan counterparts because it just so happens to be true.

> Now the story of Christ is simply a true myth: a myth working on us in the same way as the others, but with this tremendous difference that it really happened.[1]

Lewis wrote to Greeves shortly after his apologetic meeting with Tolkien and Dyson to announce, "I have just passed on from believing in God to definitely believing in Christ."[2] He added, "My long night talk with Dyson and Tolkien had a great deal to do with it."[3]

1. Hooper, *They Stand Together*, 425.

2. Ibid.

3. Ibid.

What began with Tolkien and Dyson at Addison's Walk ended with Lewis's brother Warnie on the way to the Zoo. Lewis positively crossed over into the Christian faith on September 28, 1931. Lewis and his brother Warnie were on their way to Whipsnade Zoo. Jack sat in the sidecar of Warnie's motorcycle, and before reaching the zoo had come to believe in Christ as God's Son. "When we set out I did not believe that Jesus Christ is the Son of God and when we reached the zoo I did."[4]

There are an abundance of books devoted to Lewis's conversion, and I don't mean to add to all that's been said about the spirituality of his coming to Christ. I do mean to say that his conversion to the Christian faith matters creatively because of the great change that occurred in Lewis the man and in Lewis the literary craftsman. His conversion brought renewed and unprecedented creativity. The early 1930s were the dawn of a three-decade era of writing from which came his greatest works. Lewis began to write himself to the brinks of new themes and forms, soon to try his hand at full-length novels, venturing out with new ideas, yet fond of returning to familiar forms. So to hear Lewis say to Owen Barfield, "I have written about 100 lines of a long poem in my type of Alexandrine,"[5] is to hear a seasoned writer still reaching for new creative range.

Not only did Lewis's love for poetry remain close to the heart of his creative life—as we'll continue to see—it also helped bridge his writing to his long career in Christian prose. And it was actually his affinity for poetry that influenced his first attempts at autobiography after becoming a Christian. Lewis had dabbled in the autobiographical long before his conversion. His earliest attempts came in 1922, in a poem called "Joy."[6] In "Joy," Lewis tried to capture that thread of experience that defined his early life's spiritual yearning. "Joy" was published in 1924, but Lewis's personal processing through *Sehnsucht*—desirous joy—was far from final.

There are specks of *Sehnsucht* throughout *All My Road Before Me*, in which Lewis selectively chronicled his daily activities 1922 to 1927, but the diary offers only a sliver of Lewis's life. *All My Road Before Me* does, though, open small windows to Lewis's writing life—we're allowed insights like "I tried very hard to write something today, but it was like drawing blood from a stone" and "Wrote five stanzas for the third canto of 'Dymer.'"[7] But

---

4. Lewis, *Surprised by Joy*, 223.
5. Hooper, *Collected Letters* 2.55.
6. If we don't count his childhood attempt, *My Life*, from 1907.
7. Lewis, *All My Road Before Me*, 19, 50.

its ultimate purpose seems to be to distract from the monotony—and for the atheist Lewis, possibly the perceived meaninglessness—of its author's day-to-day life:

> Decided at whatever cost of labour to start my diary rigorously again, wh[ich] has been dropped during Schools, as I think the day to day continuity helps one to see the larger movement and pay less attention to each damned day in itself . . . .[8]

He started on another autobiographical account focused on "Joy" in a fifty-eight-page prose attempt meant to explain how he moved from materialism to belief in God. In the spring of 1932, Lewis tried an autobiographical attempt at joy in verse and sent the poem to Owen Barfield. It begins,

> I will write down the portion that I understand
> Of twenty years wherein I went from to land to land.
> At many bays and harbours I put in with joy.[9]

This poem might seem insignificant, but in a survey of Lewis's creative life, it marks an important development in his writing. It was the penultimate step in a long history of revision that ended in *The Pilgrim's Regress*. Lewis wrote his autobiographical allegory in a two-week blitz of inspiration while on holiday with Greeves in Ireland. Impressively, Lewis was also at work on *The Allegory of Love*, published in 1936.

Published as *The Pilgrim's Regress: An Allegorical Apology for Christianity, Reason, and Romanticism* on May 25, 1933, Lewis instantly feared it would be a failure "at least as big a failure as *Dymer*."[10] Lewis recalled his comforting letter to Greeves upon the rejection of Arthur's novel, trying to "take heart all the things I wrote you when you were bowled over by Reid's decision on your first novel—not entirely without success."[11]

Though his writing pace was inimitable, the product was unpolished. Lewis's Bunyanesque allegory about a character named John on a journey to the island of Joy is loaded with abstract allusions, overly simple

---

8   Ibid., 246.

9. Hooper includes the only extant excerpt of Lewis's poem in Lewis's *Collected Letters* 2.78.

10. Lewis, *All My Road Before Me*, 438. While *Dymer* garnered some praise, it also earned its share of criticism. From Barfield, "The metrical level is good, the vocabulary is large: but Poetry—not a line."

11. Hooper, *Collected Letters* 2.112.

characterizations of culture, and at times a convoluted style. The book shows us a Lewis still learning how to write a novel—to be what his childhood days as a "novelist in training" portended. Perhaps more revealing, *Pilgrim's Regress* shows us a vulnerable writer in need of feedback. The novel was written in Greeves' house, shaped by his suggestions, and dedicated to him. To Greeves, Lewis wrote,

> I suppose you have no objection to my dedicating the book to you? It is yours by every right—written in your house, read to you as it was written, and celebrating (at least in the most important parts) an experience which I have more in common with you than anyone else. By the bye, you will be interested to hear that in finally revising the MS I did adopt many of your corrections, or at least made alterations where you objected. So if the book is a ghastly failure I shall always say "Ah it's this Arthur business"[12]

Lewis asked Greeves for his thoughts on instances of "confusion, bad taste, unsuccessful jokes, contradictions etc" in the novel. Greeves obliged, taking aim at Lewis's style, which opened Lewis up to elaborate on his stylistic aim and ideas in language:

> I think, I see, from your criticisms, that you like a much more correct, classical, and elaborate manner than I. I am chiefly at being idiomatic and racy, basing myself on Malory, Bunyan, and Morris, tho' without archaisms: and would usually prefer to use ten words, provided they are honest native words and idiomatically ordered, than one "literary word."[13]

In a sentence that summarizes his view of formal language in fiction, Lewis added, "To put the thing in a nutshell you want 'The man of whom I told you' and I want 'The man I told you of.'"[14] But, Lewis ended with, "there are many sentences in the P.R. which are bad by any theory of style."[15]

Greeves thought the novel rudimentary in style, yet criticized *Regress* for being overly complex in content, no doubt in part because of Lewis's saturation of contextless allusion and quotation. Defending against Greeves's accusation that the novel lacked salient simplicity, Lewis—arguing Jesus's

---

12. Ibid., 104.
13. Ibid., 89.
14. Ibid.
15. Ibid.

charge to have childlike faith as a rule for guilelessness, not simple minded-ness faith—wrote,

> I doubt if I interpret Our Lord's words quite in the same way as
> you. I think they mean that the *spirit* of man must become humble
> and trustful like a child and, like a child, *simple in motive*, i.e.
> disinterested, not scheming and "on the look out." I don't think He
> meant that adult Christians must think like children: still less that
> the processes of thought by wh[ich] people become Christians
> must be childish processes.[16]

Lewis adds that the intellectual part of his conversion was not simple, and he did not know any other way to narrate it.[17] It's not surprising, then, given Greeves's feedback, that twenty years later, in 1953, Lewis would look back on the book's style with the wisdom of a seasoned novelist:

> I don't wonder that you got fogged in Pilgrim's Regress. It was my
> first religious book and I didn't then know how to make things
> easy. I was not even trying to very much, because in those days I
> never dreamed I would become a "popular" author and hoped for
> no readers outside a small "highbrow circle."[18]

For the writer

Striking upon the right style remains the writer's duty and call. Duty because the writer must aim to write the best sentence he possibly can—impossible without finding his individual style. Call because the craft summons the writer to write as an individual, with his own voice and tone—the very ingredients of an author's style. Through each draft, through writing and rewriting, the writer becomes conscious of his style, why he prefers not to end sentences with prepositions or why those sentences tend to be compound instead of simple.

How would you describe your writing style? What books and authors have influenced your style?

Do try: In 350-400 words, write about your style. Ask yourself these questions: where did I first learn my style of writing? What exactly

16. Ibid., 93.

17. Ibid.

18. Hooper, *Collected Letters* 3.282–83.

characterizes my style? What elements of style do I insist on and which do I tend to neglect? Think about things like your voice, which verb tenses you're prone to use, and how casual or formal you tend to be. Don't overthink before beginning this small essay. Just start writing.

33

Form Is Soul

In a quote worth revisiting from his essay, "An Approach to English," fellow Oxford classmate, friend, and occasional Inkling Nevill Coghill said of his and Lewis's young literary dreams,

> We saw clearly what lay before us, a life of reading and teaching, perhaps of writing—for, as we confessed to each other very soon, we both hoped to be poets, or at least writers.[1]

Coghill recalled Lewis's regretful resignation some years later, when Lewis came to believe his aspirations to be a well-known poet wouldn't come to fruition. Lewis experienced a period of creative disenchantment, admitting, "I at last realized that I was not, after all, going to be a great man . . . ."[2] Coghill simply added, "I think he meant a great poet."[3]

Lewis, inarguably a great writer, never achieved the status of great poet. As a published author, Lewis has been and forever will be best known for his prose. But it's his extensive labors in poetry that contain some of the most exemplary paradigms for writing and the writing life. Even *The Pilgrim's Regress*, his first major work of fictive prose, is somewhat of a hybrid, a novel injected with poetry. Lewis simply couldn't get away from verse, and within his thinking on verse we find rich insight into his views on writing. In 1936, Lewis—elaborating on the exact nature and purpose

---

1. Coghill, "The Approach to English," 53.
2. Ibid.
3. Ibid.

of poetry—wrote to friend, fellow man of letters, and Catholic Monk, Dom Bede Griffiths,

> Surely the truth is that poetry is simply a special kind of speech, a way of saying things, and one can no more talk about poetry in the abstract than about "saying."[4]

Writing might be likened to speech in general, but poetry must be, Lewis contended, seen as a particular kind of speech. Poetry says something in a way that only poetry can. Poetry has no necessary bearing on what is said, since a poet might write about any topic, but poetry emphasizes *how* something is said. When poetry becomes the mode for saying a thing—about love or religion, for example—then by association it becomes a part of that thing. Regardless of the topic, the mode remains a mode.

> When what the poet is saying is religious, poetry is simply a part of religion. When what he says is simply entertaining, poetry is a form of entertainment. When what he says is wicked, poetry is simply a form of sin. Whenever one is talking, if one begins to utilize rhythm, metaphor, association etc, one is beginning to use "poetry": but the whole place of that poetry in the scheme of things depends on what you are talking about. In fact, in a sense there is no such thing as poetry. It is not an element but a mode.[5]

Not only does Lewis give poets a distinct way of seeing their art—poetry not as subject, not as object, but as a mode—we also find in his poetics a sketch of the writer's role. The writer toils in the *what* of a thing said and in the *how* that thing is said. With the element and the mode. Or, as Lewis would go on to write in A*n Experiment in Criticism*, the *logos* (something said) and the *poiema* (something made). It's the writer's task to make and remake the mode so that the element—the thing said—might be clearly, powerfully, and beautifully evident.

What might be one of the most interesting aspects of Lewis's creative life, although perhaps the least discussed, is what his process crafting both element and mode looked like. As it turns out, his ongoing relationship with poetry unfolds some of that process for us. In 1938, Lewis shared a poem with Owen Barfield that would be published as "Experiment" in 1939 and again as "Pattern" in Walter Hooper's 1964 collection, *Poems*.

---

4. Hooper, *Collected Letters* 2.200.

5. Ibid., 200–201.

Form is soul. In warmer
Seductive days, disarming
Its firmer will, the wood grows soft
And spreads its dreams to murmur;[6]

Then form returns. In warmer,
Seductive days, disarming
Its firmer will, the wood grew soft
And put forth dreams to murmur.[7]

We immediately notice Lewis's revisions to the first line. Present being verb, "is," changed to the more active "returns" and given a successive order with "then." While the poem is about seasons, Lewis, in his eternal interest in the craft, has in mind the ideas on writing and form he shared with Griffiths. "Form is soul" was Lewis's way of working out the relationship between subject and mode. "Grows" to "grew"; "spreads its dreams" to "put forth dreams": these might seem like minor redactions, but each revision rehearses the kind of ministration Lewis devoted to writing, both mode and word.

Lewis returned to poetry between—and while—writing his published prose works.[8] His process remained exacting. While he would let months, even years, pass before revising an old "finished" poem, Lewis would return to a poem to rethink and vivisect with remarkable precision. In the preface to *On Stories*, Walter Hooper said that

> Except for his academic works, Lewis never wrote more than a single draft of his novels, which indeed suggests that the stories were worked out in his head before he put pen to paper.[9]

6. Ibid., 230.

7. Lewis, *Poems*, 79.

8. Just one example of Lewis's activity as a poet would be the four poems Lewis sent to an anthology published by Cambridge University Press, titled *Fear No More: A Book of Poems for the Present Time by Living English Poets* in 1940: "I have contributed four poems to an anthology which the Cambridge University Press is bringing out on a most original plan: i.e. no author's names at all. It will be very interesting to see what reviewers make of it." Hooper, *Collected Letters* 2.356. In addition, I have already mentioned Don King's seminal work on Lewis's poetry. I defer to his scholarship again here as the most complete study of that topic with this distinction: what King does so well—and what I am here trying to do on a much smaller scale—is reveal the mind and methods of an eminent wordsmith. See also Lewis's letter to poet and regular correspondent Ruth Pitter. Lewis includes "The Birth of Language," "To Charles Williams," and "On Being Human": see Hooper, *Collected Letters* 2.725–28.

9. Hooper, "Preface," *On Stories*, xvii.

This almost superhuman ability to write a final draft with one fell swoop might be true of some of Lewis's prose, but behind his poetry stands a more methodical craftsman. Poems like "The Atomic Bomb," which Lewis sent to Owen Barfield before it was revised and published by *The Spectator* in 1945 as "On the Atomic Bomb: Metrical Experiment," suggests that rewriting was writing, that the process matters as much as the product.

So: you have found an engine
Of injury that angels
Might dread. The world plunges,
Shies, snorts and curvets like a horse in danger.
Well: comfort her with fondling, [Lewis changed to "Then comfort her
    with fondlings"]
With kindly *words* and handl*ings*, [changed to "word" and "handling"]
But *never* believe blindly [changed to "But do not"]
This way or that. Both fears and hopes are swindlers.
What's here to dread? For mortals
Both hurt and death were certain
Already: our light-hearted
Hopes sentenced from the first to final thwarting. [Lewis changed to
    "Hopes from the first sentenced to final thwarting."]
This *makes* no huge advance in [changed to "marks"]
The dance of Death. His pincers
Were grim before with chances
Of cold, fire, suffocation, Ogpu, cancer.
Nor hope that this last blunder
Will end our woes by rending
Tellus herself asunder
In one wide flash that fades and leaves no cinder. [Lewis changed to "All
    gone in one bright flash like dryest tinder."]
Alas!, no mortal gadget [Lewis changed to "As if your puny gadget"]
Will dodge the terrible logic [changed to "Could"]
Of history. The long, tragic [changed to "Of history! No; the tragic"]
Tale ends not till the Master comes to judge it. [Lewis changed to "Road
    will go on, new generations trudge it"]

Lewis included a *Varia lectio,* a "variant reading," to the last stanza in his edition to Barfield: "The long, tragic / Road will go on, new generations trudge it."[10] A week after Lewis sent "The Atomic Bomb" to Barfield, he

10. Hooper, *Collected Letters* 2.688. The revised poem appears in Lewis's collected *Poems,* 64.

sent yet another rewritten copy to writer and friend Cecil Harwood with a newly written last stanza that read:

> Narrow and long it stretches,
> Wretched for him who marches
> Eyes front. He never catches
> A glimpse of the fields each side, the happy orchards.[11]

To poet and affectionate friend Ruth Pitter, Lewis sent two versions, labeled "A Version" and "B Version," of a poem called "Two Kinds of Memory" in a letter that begins,

> Dear Miss Pitter —
> I want advice.[12]

Lewis's humility toward writing is apparent. And his revision, an open process. Not only did Lewis write—and rewrite—with a belief that good writing was drafted writing, he also put himself in the way of writerly wisdom, willing to draft on the advice of others:

> I have written two different poems and all my friends disagree, some violently championing A and some B, and some neither. Will you give a vote? Firstly, is either any good? Secondly, if so, which is the good one?[13]

Pitter preferred "B."

For the writer

In writing, what matters most isn't only what it is you want to say. As a wordsmith, how you say what you want to say matters as much. The *how* is form. Finding form is about balance. It's that symmetrical fit of element to mode, subject to genre, the thing said (the *logos*) to the thing made (the *poiema*). The writer realizes how form can change content, how form can become soul.

What literary forms are you most drawn to? What is it about those forms that move or convince you?

11. Ibid., 692.

12. Ibid., 758.

13. Ibid; see also Lewis's letter to Pitter from July 6, 1947 in *Collected Letters* 2.790–95.

Do try: Choose a theme. It can be anything. Love, grace, God, regret, pain, trauma, prayer, choice. Now, spend a few minutes deciding what form best suits your theme. Finally, take at least an hour to write on your theme in your form of choice. While it's only natural to put what you want to say first, try to focus on form. Think about how your form can best say what needs to be said.

34

Crisp as Grape Nuts, Hard as a Hammer, Clear as Glass

The Lewis that creatively conspired with Greeves, drafted with Barfield, and solicited from Pitter was a relational writer. Not just in his younger, more formative, years, but throughout his entire writing life, Lewis graciously invited feedback on his writing and positively effused with thoughts on others' work. Writing was, for Lewis, as relational as it was refining. As his correspondence with fellow writers shows, he was an iron sharpening iron.

When Lewis read Owen Barfield's unpublished poem "The Tower," he wrote Barfield with detailed feedback and heaping praise, "I have no doubt at all that you are engaged in writing one of the really great poems of the world."[1]

Lewis particularly admired Barfield's ability to reconcile those things previously incompatible. Barfield was able to capture the "labyrinthine fidgey world of the inner mine" while simultaneously displaying a Miltonian or Marlownian prowess for poetic soaring and winged "movement."[2] To Lewis, Barfield displayed the rare ability to poeticize the passion of a creature "that lives after its back is broken" through melodiously versed philosophy, placing Barfield among the "very great people."[3]

---

1. Hooper, *Collected Letters* 3.1505.
2. Ibid.
3. Ibid.

But as thrilled as Lewis was with Barfield's "Tower," the poem still needed some work: "Two parts as a whole seem inferior," Lewis began his critique, continuing, "pictures are not really your long suit."[4] Rather than real or vivid, Lewis found Barfield's use of images "literary and uninteresting."

When Lewis read fellow Inkling Charles Williams's wildly unique novel, *Descent into Hell*, he offered a review that both challenged and affirmed Williams's prose:

> I hope this doesn't sound patronizing—in sheer writing I think you have gone up, as we examiners say, a whole class. Chapter II is in my opinion your high water mark so far. Your have completely overcome a certain flamboyance which I always thought your chief dangers: this is crisp as grape nuts, hard as a hammer, clear as glass. I am a little worried in the Wentworth part by the tendency to Gertrude Steinisms (eaves eves, guard card, etc).[5]

Lewis valued concrete, clear, certain writing—the kind Williams hadn't always produced. Williams tended to write with a particular ostentatiousness. He was prone to overwritten assonance, which, unfortunately, reminded Lewis of modernist writer Gertrude Stein's style. Though, on the whole, Lewis found the writing in *Descent into Hell* lucid and exact.

Lewis poured through Williams's novels, praising his prose when opportunity arose. While reading Williams's *He Came Down from Heaven*, Lewis felt obliged to say, "It is a work thickly inlaid with patins of bright gold—."[6]

Sentences in Williams like, "He does not exist primarily for us" and "All that could be said would be that they had not *yet* happened," struck Lewis. These were passages that could very well "straddle across the ages."[7] What was it about Williams's writing that elicited such praise from Lewis? Chiefly, clarity: "It's so *clear*, which at one time I should never have expected a book of yours to be."[8]

To some desirous writers, Lewis's feedback cut to the quick. To author Vera Matthews, who sent a short story titled "Nabob" for feedback, Lewis

4. Ibid., 1506.

5. Hooper, *Collected Letters* 2.219.

6. Ibid., 227.

7. Ibid.

8. Ibid., 228.

paid the compliment of naked truth and perfectly honest judgment—"I don't think the story, as it stands, will do"[9]—while assuring Matthews that

> its partial failure does not prove (this is what you most want to know) an absence of literary talent. What is wrong with the story is due to inexperience.

Lewis did try to follow his medicine with a teaspoon of sugar: "There is nothing amatereurish about the actual writing and you have, I think, the gift of ordonnance [general presentation]."[10]

To all writers who sought his counsel, Lewis generously offered his advice and time for the sharpening of their craft. At times, he would respond with an almost line-by-line edit, announcing his suggested revisions down to the paragraph number, page, and phrase: to Helen Calkins, author of *India Looks*, he wrote,

> Here are a few notes wh[ich] you may or may not find worth considering.
> P. 3. para 4. Trojan heroes etc. Does it matter that of those you mention only Hector was on the Trojan side?
> P 4. Leaf's poem. Dazzle and the stress. Are you sure it isn't dazzle and stress?
> P. 45 First sentence. Again, conveys no clear meaning to me. Simplify! Simplify![11]

Lewis had a long relationship in letters with Catholic nun and prolific writer Sister Penelope. Lewis read her works with delight and didn't hesitate to reply. After reading Sister Penelope's *The Coming of the Lord*, Lewis responded:

> I think it is the best book you have yet done, and the best theological book by anyone I have read for a long time. (You are, among other things, the only person I ever met who gives me real light on the Old Testament). Chapter VIII now convinces me completely.[12]

Lewis rarely offered praise without following it with prescriptions for how to improve the writing. Even the most capable writers, like Sister Penelope, received advice: "Now for a few tiny flaws, or what I think to be

---

9. Hooper, *Collected Letters* 3.167.

10. Ibid.

11. Ibid., 176. Lewis offered this detailed sort of epistolary feedback on several occasions to several writers.

12. Ibid., 316.

such."[13] Lewis could be a fierce editor. He had no problems helping authors hone their manuscripts through "amputation," as he put it. As he wrote to Colin Hardie, who had sent over an essay called "The Myth of Paris," the "business of a cutter is to cut."[14]

Sheldon Vanauken, Lewis admirer, eventual epistolary friend, and author of the deeply moving *A Severe Mercy*, sent Lewis six sonnets he called the *Oxford Sonnets*. In a letter from June 1952, Lewis replied,

> The sonnets, though in a manner which will win few hearers at the moment (drat all fashions) are really very remarkable. The test is that I found myself at once forgetting all the personal biographical interest and reading them as poetry. The image of sand is *real* imagination. . . . The second quatrain of The Gap is tip-top argument—and then the ground sinking behind. Excellent.[15]

And to poet Phoebe Hesketh:

> You are a superb phrase-maker: "the bell-noised stream" and "infant fists of fern" on p. 8—"Shack-Age" on p. 9—"caged in comic bars of camoflage" on 39—and the really unbearable two lines about Time's finger & the evening train on p.81. Ugh![16]

Sister Penelope, Vanauken, and Hesketh kept up correspondence with Lewis for years. Lewis stayed faithful to these literary relationships, each a means of spurring and honing the writing craft—though it is safe to say that Lewis did most of the spurring and his recipients enjoyed the lion's share of honing.

And Lewis spared his students no vivisection, reading their papers with the same scrutiny he showed aspiring writers. George Bailey, an undergraduate student at Magdalen College under Lewis's tutelage during the mid-40s, recalled Lewis's predictable feedback on student papers. If a student's essay was good, then Lewis's response would write,

> There is a good deal in what you say.[17]

If average,

> There is something in what you say.

13. Ibid., 317.
14. Ibid., 113.
15. Ibid., 196.
16. Ibid., 233–34.
17. Bailey, "In the University," 81.

And if the essay was bad, Lewis wrote,

> There may be something in what you say.[18]

Other comments included, "Too much straw and not enough bricks" and the more colorful, "Not with Brogans, please, slippers are in order when you proceed to make a literary point."[19] These recollections of Lewis and the Oxford tutorial system shed more light on Lewis's approach to writing. Lewis demanded that a writer bring quality thinking and a host of meaningful ideas to bear in his writing. There must be weight within the words.

Lewis saved his praise for few essays. "Much of that was very well said," was the best Bailey ever received from Lewis. There were certain qualities Lewis looked for in an essay and praised when he found them. Once Bailey used the word "bracing" to describe the poetry of Dryden, a word choice Lewis "spent five minutes praising."[20] Lewis was especially "quick to notice any excellence of usage."[21]

It is fitting that what Bailey describes as "the most important point about the tutorial system in general and Lewis's use of it in particular" is that "'what you say' is either 'well said' or not."[22] Bailey's assessment seconds what Lewis so often claimed makes for good writing. Good writing will simply sound like good writing. Sound mattered a great deal to Lewis. It marked good writing. Lewis taught writing by reading the paper aloud with the assumption that in order for the undergraduate to write well, he "must write so that when he reads aloud his tutor will understand without being obliged to request the repetition of a sentence or a phrase."[23]

If a tutor had to ask the student to repeat a sentence or phrase, then there was a fatal flaw in the writing. "As far as I know," Bailey notes, "Lewis simply declined to request repetition."[24] If clarity didn't define the first draft, then it was a failed attempt.

While "immediate intelligibility," or clarity, was Lewis's first commandment of writing, it was not his only. Bailey lays his finger on the pulse of Lewis's writing value system. Good writing is not only clear; it's also

---

18. Ibid.
19. Ibid.
20. Ibid.
21. Ibid.
22. Ibid., 81–82.
23. Ibid., 82.
24. Ibid.

interesting and lively. Timing is key. Both in lectures and in writing: "Lewis was a master in the art of putting thing pungently, of forming and timing statements so that they were unforgettable."[25]

For the writer

Criticism—like Lewis's critiques of others' work—gives us a language for writing. We learn about ourselves as writers and our writing tendencies when we are forced to articulate our ideas about others' writing. Forming a critical response about someone's writing is one of the primary ways a writer knows what works and what doesn't—which image evokes and which falls flat or why a sentence sings or clunks awkwardly along. A writer isn't one who only puts her best words on her page. A writer also helps diagnose whether another's words are best and belong on their page.

What ideas, terms, or approaches you have learned from evaluating another's work? Have you learned anything specific about your style from either giving or getting criticism? If so, list and explain. What kind of helpful vocabulary does criticism offer your approach to writing?

Do try: Write a work of criticism. Choose any poem, short story, or essay and write an analysis. Be detailed and specific. Try to imitate some of Lewis's critique in this chapter. Ask of whatever work you read the kinds of questions Lewis asked. Look for the issues Lewis did.

25. Ibid.

35

Not a Vestige of Real Creativity

Writing is creativity's conduit. To discuss any particular writer's relationship with writing, we must go beyond craft—while never leaving it—and get down to how that writer viewed creativity. What makes C. S. Lewis the writer's writer—the heart of what I wanted to get to in a book on Lewis and writing—is his rare, remarkable creative capacity. His prose is exemplary, his ability to move through an argument incomparable, and his range across genres unparalleled among his contemporaries, but the marvel—indeed, the genius—of Lewis's writing lies in what might called his creativology, his study of how creativity worked in and on the writer.

Lewis and Sister Penelope's exchanges form an anthology of creative theory and practical advice on writing. It was with Sister Penelope that Lewis articulated a string of writerly insights into creativity and craft:

> "Creation" as applied to human authorship seems to me an entirely misleading term. We make ["with regard to what lies at hand"] i.e. we re-arrange elements He has provided. There is not a vestige of real creativity de novo in us. Try to imagine a new primary colour, a third sex, a fourth dimension, or even a monster wh[ich] does not consist of bits of existing animals stuck together! Nothing happens. And that surely is why our works (as you said) never mean to others quite what we intended: because we are re-creating elements made by Him and already containing His meanings. Because of those divine meanings in our materials it is impossible

we sh[oul]d ever know the whole meaning of our own works, and the meaning we never intended may be the best and truest one.[1]

Lewis's thinking here is liberating to the writer. For the writer, there is no creation *ex nihilo*. The writer's imagination works with what *is*, according to Lewis, and what is has innate, God-given meaning. The writer is freed from total originality. This is especially comforting since total originality, he wrote in *Mere Christianity*, is an utter myth:

> Even in literature and art, no man who bothers about originality will ever be original: whereas if you simply try to tell the truth (without caring twopence how often it has been told before) you will, nine times out of ten, become original without ever having noticed it.[2]

Unoriginality is somewhat of a gift to the writer. Any imaginative element used by the writer comes endowed with meaning from the Originator of all meaning. God gives the words, images, and themes to the writer, and it's He, not the writer, who ultimately determines how that meaning will work its way into readers' lives. Regarding the manner in which creativity works in an author's creation of a book, Lewis went on to say to Sister Penelope:

> Writing a book is much less like creation than it is like planting a garden or begetting a child: in all three cases we are only entering as one cause into a causal stream which works, so to speak, it its own way. I w[oul]d not wish it to be otherwise. If one c[oul]d really create in the strict sense w[oul]d one not find one had created a sort of Hell?[3]

Writing works as a cause in a process already caused by the creative impulse. Creativity brings the writer out of the self—a self-enclosed kind of hell incapable of generating anything beyond itself—because creativity flows like an eternally endless stream. The writer has only to play his part, to be a co-creative cause in the continuous movement of creativity.

Lewis's view of creativity determined how he saw himself and how he saw his writing. Literature, Lewis thought, must be a creative conduit through which passes existing ideas. Because the writer wasn't responsible for—or even capable of—original thought, his role was more of a translator

---

1. Hooper, *Collected Letters* 2.555.
2. Lewis, *Mere Christianity*, 226.
3. Hooper, *Collected Letters* 2.555.

for pre-existent truths. Not only is the writer to act as translator, he must also translate existent ideas into accessible language, into vernacular.

> I agree that it is essential for all "literature" it issues to its members to be a *translation* into the actual current speech of the people. . . . But of course I can't write a book for workers. I know nothing at all of the realities of factory life. If one of you will write the book, I will translate it: i.e. instead of a book by me edited by you, you need a book by you edited by me.[4]

Lewis accepted his role as a translator, but desired a somewhat different creative role. Lewis continues, "People praise me as a 'translator', but what I want is to be the founder of a school of 'translation.'"[5] Lewis desired writers who saw their creative capacity in light of their unoriginality.

> I am nearly forty-seven. Where are my successors? Anyone can learn to do it if they wish. It only involves first writing down in ordinary theological college English exactly what you want to say and then treating that just as you treated a piece of English set for Greek prose school.[6]

The writer's work doesn't need to be novel, but rather, banal. The writer translates creativity into plain craft. And the inability to do so is both a problem in creative understanding and style—"It is also a v. good discipline because nine times out of ten the bit you can't turn into Vernacular turns out to be the bit which hadn't any clear meaning to begin with."[7]

For the writer

The writer lives, moves, and has his being in creativity. But how a writer views creativity greatly determines how he sees his role as a writer and how he sees his art. Thinking about creativity—working toward a creativology—deepens the writer's sense of self; shapes the sense of vocation; affects what the writer writes. Creativity always translates into craft. The good writer keeps his head in the space of that translation.

4. Ibid., 674.
5. Ibid.
6. Ibid.
7. Ibid.

What is your view of creativity, your creativology? How has—or how can—your view of creativity shaped how you see yourself as a writer and your work? How does the writer tap into, channel, or exercise creativity?

Do try: In at least 400 words, write a position paper about creativity. Define it. Narrate your experience with it. Explain how it works in the writing process.

36

An Idea and Then an Itch

In reply to an ongoing epistolary discussion about the nature of artistic conscience—that inner moral judge that determines which works are worth writing and which works are not—Lewis wrote to Dorothy Sayers that the desire to write has little bearing on the quality of the work written. Of course, the writer shouldn't write dishonest work. But honest work, Lewis argued, has little to do with the itch to write, an idea that seemed to Lewis "like making 'being in love' the only reason for going on with a marriage."[1]

To write honestly, the writer couldn't trust the impulse alone. Excitement doesn't necessarily make for noble writing. Valuable work might very well come from disciplined, unexcited writing. Lewis continued:

> in my experience the desire has no constant ratio to the value of the work done. My own frequent uneasiness comes from another source—the fact that apologetic work is so dangerous to one's own faith. A doctrine never seems dimmer to me than when I have just successfully defended it.[2]

Lewis suggested that what made for honest writing wasn't whether or not the writer possessed a certain degree of correlating desire—as if more desire made for better writing and less desire, worse. Rather—and here he's referring to his apologetic writing—a greater threat to honest writing is the

1. Hooper, *Collected Letters* 2.730.
2. Ibid.

loss of luster a truth suffers once the writer has handled it. In other words, dangerous writing—that closest to artistic dishonesty—dims the light on its subject. Writing about a subject should do nothing to diminish what that subject means to the writer, as apologetics had the tendency to do with Lewis's faith. This makes writing, particularly good, honest writing, an exercise of the will. The writer simply pushes on with the work despite how he feels.

Lewis's exchange with Sayers suggests to writers a deeper value system for judging their work. The writer's integrity has little or nothing to do with how much desire she felt writing it and everything to do with her relationship to the topic. This is interesting given Lewis's own sensitivity to the desire to write. To poet Martyn Skinner, author of *Two Colloquies*, Lewis said about writing's addictive appeal,

> The right mood for a new poem doesn't come so often now as it used to. *Ink* is a deadly drug. One wants to write. I cannot shake off the addiction.[3]

Not at all bashful about the sheer power of writing's allure, Lewis described desire as a creative catalyst, a fundamental part of the writing process. Very much the writer's mantra, "one wants to write" captures the creative rumblings that moved Lewis from essay to poem, book to written sermon. Lewis once said that the ideas for his books came from an incentivized compulsion: "The 'incentive' for my books has always been the usual one—an idea and then an itch or lust to write."[4]

Ideas came to Lewis strikingly and in the most interesting ways. Lewis's popular *The Screwtape Letters* is a good example. Lewis wrote to his brother Warnie on July 20, 1940, recalling hearing Hitler over the radio the night before. Lewis was surprised at how moved he was by Hitler's rhetoric, confessing,

> it is a positive revelation to me how while the speech lasts it is impossible not to waver just a little. I should be useless as a schoolmaster or a policeman. Statements which I *know* to be untrue all but convince me, at any rate for the moment, if only the man says them unflinchingly.[5]

---

3. Hooper, *Collected Letters* 3.56–57.
4. Hooper, *Collected Letters* 2.830.
5. Ibid., 425.

The idea of diabolically convincing discourse took root. It was shortly after, in the Communion service at Holy Trinity Church, Headington Quarry, that the idea for a book bloomed.

> Before the service was over—one could wish these things came more seasonably—I was struck by an idea for a book which I think might be both useful and entertaining. It would be called *As One Devil to Another* and would consist of letters from an elderly retired devil to a young devil who has just started work on his first "patient." The idea would be to give all the psychology of temptation from the *other* point of view.[6]

The itch immediately followed the idea. Lewis likely finished *The Screwtape Letters*—a title Lewis came to favor over *As One Devil to Another*—by Christmas of 1940.

Not all of Lewis's ideas turned into itches quite so quickly. The creative process took longer with some books, though it was no less compulsive. The idea for Lewis's fantastic theological fiction *The Great Divorce* developed more slowly. Lewis first got the idea of the "Refrigerium" from seventeenth-century Anglican writer and cleric Jeremy Taylor's sermon "Christ's Advent to Judgement." Taylor said about the Refrigerium—held to be a time of refreshment and spiritual ease for the damned—"the perishing souls in hell may have sometimes remission and refreshment, like the fits of an intermitting fever."[7]

Walter Hooper points out that Lewis collected his ideas about the Refrigerium from verses like Psalm 65:12 in the Vulgate—the Latin translation of the Bible—and Lewis's more nascent thinking about freewill and the purpose of hell itself in stopping the reproduction of evil.[8] Once the idea converted to itch, Lewis started on the book, sharing sections of it with the Inklings, working at turning itch into ink. Lewis finished the book by the summer of 1944, almost fifteen years after first feeling its "incentive."

For the writer

Writing is largely about desire. From idea to itch, the writer translates abstract inspiration into ink. This is the writer's life. One wants to write.

---

6. Ibid., 426.

7. Taylor, *Whole Works* 5.45.

8. Hooper, *C. S. Lewis: Companion & Guide*, 281.

To wait for creative impulse, to savor it when it comes, to be someone on whom nothing is lost. Desire and ideas incentivize the writing act, creating an impulse. The writer then has to move from that impulse. To move from Hitler to *Screwtape*. From the Refrigerium to *The Great Divorce*.

Do you have an "itch" to write? Describe it. How do you go from idea to desire? How do you practically go about acting on that desire?

Do try: Write an informal journal entry—aim to write reflectively and beautifully, while remembering to be plain and personal—about the writing itch. Reflect on how an idea turns into that creative itch. Focus on one particular moment of writerly desire. Describe it. What did you learn about yourself from it? How did you practically move from itch to ink?

37

One Never Knows What One's in For

Perhaps one of the most valuable lessons Lewis teaches writers is that the desire to write must eventually take on a discerning form. The idea and itch aren't enough. Writers must get on with the business of writing, determining what to write and what not to write. This is the *ink* part of the writing process. Lewis's life is a fascinating study of the balance between ingenious imagination and the particulars of process—writers do well to remember one aspect of his relationship to writing when considering the other.

The sci-fi author, imaginative apologist, epistolary mind behind *The Screwtape Letters*, and creator of Aslan is the same writer who devoted valuable time debating with one Mrs. E. L. Baxter on why he used the word "precocity." Ever-conscious of his style and always equipped with an answer for it, Lewis replied to a letter from Baxter,

> About precocity, this isn't a change in my style. I have always had two ways of writing, one for the people (to be used in works of popularized theology) and one that never aimed at simplicity (in scholarly or imaginative works). I don't think I could, or ought, to write romances & fantasies in the style of my broadcast talks. And I'm impenitent about *dindle*. You saw at once what it meant and so I've added a lovely word to your vocabulary. Why do you object?[1]

Lewis lets us into his philosophy of writing, comprised in part by his rhetorical aim. For the people—the laity, the proletariat—Lewis wrote

1. Hooper, *Collected Letters* 2.797.

accessibly. Works like *The Problem of Pain* and *Mere Christianity* were written simply and by the strong hand of Lewis's logical lead. Lewis wrote other works, those "never aimed at simplicity," for specialized academic audiences. In those books, he changed his rhetorical aim. Lewis said that *The Allegory of Love*, his treatise on allegorical love in Medieval and Renaissance literature, was "mainly for people who will want to know where they must look to verify my facts."[2] With those audiences, Lewis could write at a higher level, taking license to reveal the complexity of his thinking and advance complicated arguments.

With different authorial intent and divergent rhetorical aim comes varied vocabulary. Lewis wisely responded that some books can't be written in some styles. Fantasies force a certain feel. Sci-fi prescribes a certain style. Apologetics, another entirely. If a wise writer uses certain words, like "precocity" or "dindle," about which Lewis was unrepentant, they are called for by the audience and rhetorical occasion. Choosing a term for one work but not another isn't a change in style, as Baxter suspected with Lewis, but rather the practice of discernment. "Eternal vivisector" works for *A Grief Observed*, but not for *The Horse and His Boy*.

Lewis's writerly self-awareness stands as a lesson to authors: know yourself, know your style, and know your strengths. Lewis had an uncanny knack for staying within his creative lane. Prose, for example, both essay and story, came as naturally to him as to any essayist or novelist who ever lived. Humphrey Carpenter, in his seminal work on the Inklings, said of Lewis's writing process, "The writing of stories in prose came almost incredibly easy to Lewis."[3] Like Hooper, Carpenter testified to Lewis's ability to plow through prose: "He worked fast, managed to write almost everything in one draft, and never made more than minimal revisions." Whereas Lewis tended to struggle with verse, which he would revise relentlessly over long periods of time, he made quick work of prose. About writing prose, Carpenter recalled Lewis saying, "It's such fun after sweating over verse, like free-wheeling."[4]

Even in "free-wheeling" there were times when Lewis knew his ideas exceeded his writing's strengths. Again, responding to Mrs. Baxter—and on this occasion, Mr. Baxter—on the subject of children's stories and Christian

---

2. Ibid., 173.

3. Carpenter, *The Inklings*, 47.

4. Ibid.

themes, Lewis confessed a failure: "I have tried one myself but it was, by the unanimous verdict of my friends, so bad that I destroyed it."[5]

Despite his incredible ability, Lewis knew his limitations. There were some kinds of literature in which he didn't excel. For example, Lewis once wrote, "the short story is not my Form at all."[6] We've already seen that Lewis's creative process—wisely—included knowing when to quit a project. At times, even with those genres in which Lewis was already published, he quit a work because he couldn't quite pull it off, such as a science fiction story called "Forms of Things Unknown," which he never published. It seems that Lewis just couldn't bring the book down to the level of a general readership. Friend and biographer Roger Green thought that readers wouldn't understand it. Though Lewis planned to revise and simplify the book, he ultimately abandoned it.[7]

A writer's sense of self can serve as a kind of safeguard against writing the wrong things or spending too much wondering whether she should continue writing the wrong thing. That same sense of self, which Lewis so clearly possessed, also helps move the writer deeper into those works she should write. Writing to Sister Penelope, Lewis shared a bit about the process behind his book *Miracles*:

> I've written about 6 chapters of the book on Miracles. Did I tell you that this attempt to write on the Supernatural has turned many chapters into sort of hymns on Nature! One never knows what one's in for when one starts thinking.[8]

Way leads to way when writing, Lewis suggests, but only when the writer knows which way he's made for. Lewis's work on the supernatural led to writing about nature because Lewis had for so long—going all the way back to *Spirits in Bondage*!—thought about the relationship between nature and the divine. *Miracles*, a work of apologetics, falls into one of the categories Lewis described to Mrs. Baxter—that is to say, it was in Lewis's writing wheelhouse, precisely the kind of book Lewis was made to write.

5. Hooper, *Collected Letters* 2.802.

6. Hooper, *Collected Letters* 3.165.

7. Green and Hooper, *C. S. Lewis*, 180–81.

8. Hooper, *Collected Letters* 2.590–91.

For the writer

Good writers cultivate creative discernment. They figure out what they're great at, good at, and what they never need write again. Good writers tend to stay within their lane, continually returning to that writing for which they feel best suited. The writer who sinks into her sense of self knows what to write and knows how she wants to write—knows when to use *precocity* or *dindle*. The writer with a strong sense of self also knows when to stop on a project and when to surrender to whatever unknown one's in for.

What kind of writer are you? What kind of writing do you feel best suited for? How does your sense of self help determine your style?

Do try: Write about 1) the kind of writing that brings you the most life, or 2) the kind of writing that you're most talented in. Work on defining your identity as a writer. Think about how your identity as a writer determines your writing style. No word count, just write. Don't stop until you've said all you need to say.

38

A Thing Inside Him Pawing to Get Out

I've called C. S. Lewis a writer's writer not because he was prolific, nor because he wrote in so many genres, but because he spent so much time writing about writing. In "It All Began with a Picture," Lewis revealed the creative origins of his Narnia Chronicles and Ransom trilogy:

> All my seven Narnian books, and my three science-fiction books, began with seeing pictures in my head. At first they were not a story, just pictures. The *Lion* all began with a picture of a Faun carrying an umbrella and parcels in a snowy wood. This picture had been in my mind since I was about sixteen. Then one day, when I was about forty, I said to myself: "Let's try to make a story about it."[1]

That Lewis's imagination was mysteriously sparked by an image of a faun carrying an umbrella and parcels in a snowy wood says something about the unpredictable nature of creative inspiration and how ideas develop years before actualization. Aslan emerged from imaginative imagery and brought a story behind him.

> At first I had very little idea how the story would go. But then suddenly Aslan came bounding into it. . . . But once He was there He pulled the whole story together, and soon He pulled the six other Narnian stories in after Him.[2]

1. Lewis, "It All Began with a Picture," 53.
2. Ibid.

Aslan's arrival was quite unexpected. Mere months before Aslan bounded into Lewis's imagination, Lewis thought his best writing lay behind him. In one of his "Latin letters"—so called because Lewis wrote them in Latin—from 1949, Lewis wrote to Don Giovanni Calabria of his waned passion for writing,

> As for my own work, I would not wish to deceive you with vain hope. I am now in my fiftieth year. I feel my zeal for writing, and whatever talent I originally possessed, to be decreasing; nor (I believe) do I please my readers as I used to. My house is unquiet and devastated by women's quarrels.[3]

By the time Lewis wrote to Calabria in 1949, four years had passed since he had written a story. The last Ransom novel, *That Hideous Strength*, was published in 1945. Lewis was less than certain that another book might come:

> if it shall please God that I write more books, blessed be He. If it shall not please Him, again, blessed by He. Perhaps it will be the most wholesome thing for my soul that I lose both fame and skill lest I were to fall into that evil disease, vainglory.[4]

Incredibly, around five months after the letter to Don Giovanni, Lewis had completed *The Lion, the Witch and the Wardrobe*.[5] Though not written at the same pace of *The Pilgrim's Regress*, Lewis penned *The Lion, the Witch and the Wardrobe* quickly. Tolkien thought the book was "very hastily written" with "inconsistencies and loose ends."[6] Aslan simply couldn't wait. The author known for his works of airtight argument owes one of his most famous books to the unpredictability of imaginative material rising up to the point of creative impulse. Writing for Lewis often worked that way—image and impulse both longing for a form.

> In the Author's mind there bubbles up every now and then the material for a story. For me it invariably begins with mental

3. Hooper, *Collected Letters* 2.905.

4. Ibid., 906.

5. Hooper notes that Lewis might have been stuck and that "the story remained where it was until the early months of 1949." It is possible, Hooper says, that Lewis had made progress on *The Lion, the Witch and the Wardrobe* by the time he visited Roger Lancelyn Green in March of 1949. Green wrote in his diary on March 10, "He read me two chapters of a story for children he is writing," which "he had read to Tolkien." Cf. Green and Hooper, *C. S. Lewis: A Biography*, 309; Hooper, *Collected Letters* 2.923.

6. Carpenter, *Inklings*, 224.

pictures. This ferment leads to nothing unless it is accompanied with the longing for a Form: verse or prose, short story, novel, play or what not. When these two things click you have the Author's impulse complete. It is now a thing inside him pawing to get out. He longs to see this bubbling stuff pouring into that Form as the housewife longs to see the new jam pouring into the clean jam jar. This nags him all day long and gets in the way of his work and his sleep and his meals. It's like being in love.[7]

For the writer

So much of writing is about gestation and bringing forth. The writer mulls, then makes. That indefinite period of rumination should be cherished. All that the writer is and all he creates begins during that time. Staying attuned to insistent mental images poises the writer to create when the time comes. Once these long periods of imaginative incubation lead to impulse, it's time for the writer to long for a form. Find the right way to say what's for so long been unsaid. The writer never knows when that thing that's pawing to get out might come bounding onto the page.

In the past, how have creative ideas come to you? Have you experienced the kind of imaginative bubbling that Lewis described? Any images or ideas pawing to get out?

Do try: Think about an image, idea, or truth that's stayed with you for a while. Think about what form would best suit your image. Then, write on it. Take any creative direction you want, but try to let the image drive the writing.

7. Lewis, "Sometimes Fairy Stories May Say Best What's to be Said," 57–58.

39

Forgiven for Writing Only Two
Kinds of Books

For an Oxford don to write the kind of books that Lewis would become popularly known for was improper. To the Oxford elite, Lewis's academic literary work was expected, his dabbling in poetry was tolerable, but his popular Christian projects were not to be condoned. As Green and Hooper have said,

> In Oxford you are forgiven for writing only two kinds of books. You may write books on your own subject whatever that is, literature or science, or history. And you may write detective stories because all dons at some time get the flu, and they have to have something to read in bed. But what you are not forgiven is writing popular works, such as Jack did on theology, and especially if they win international success as his did.[1]

We can't quite understand Lewis's writing life until we appreciate how unacceptable his books were to so many. Lewis's incessant imagination and daring nature when it came to publication pushed the bounds of Oxford's literary license. Lewis's writing life was caught between professional peer expectations and his desire to write what he wanted. By and through the 1940s, what Lewis wanted to write often went against those peer expectations. When Lewis published *The Screwtape Letters*—the very kind of book Lewis's friends hated—he had "Fellow of Magdalen College, Oxford"

---

1. Green and Hooper, *C. S. Lewis: A Biography*, 340.

printed on the title page. The response was less than positive—"Many of his colleagues were outraged. This was a best-seller. He was employed as a literary scholar, not a popular evangelist!"[2]

There wasn't room at Oxford for a daytime literary scholar moonlighting as a Christian public intellectual. Indeed, on those books Lewis had a heart to write, he worked under heavy creative scrutiny:

> Owen Barfield told me that his friend Jack Lewis received much criticism for his preaching, teaching, and writing on Christian topics. . . . Being neither a theologian nor an ordained clergyman, had no business communicating these subjects to the public.[3]

Even some fellow Inklings—the intellectual community who met regularly through the 1930s and 40s, comprised of J. R. R. Tolkien, Charles Williams, Owen Barfield, Hugo Dyson—criticized some of Lewis's most famous works. Given to conversation about matters ranging from the theological to the literary, the Inklings served as a writing group—a truly reductionist way of describing any group with the likes of Tolkien and Williams, and co.—for Lewis.[4] The relationships that constituted the Inklings gave Lewis a creative community, friendships that would foster works like Tolkien's *The Hobbit* and Lewis's *The Problem of Pain*.

> We had a very pleasant evening drinking gin and limejuice and reading our recent chapters to each other—his from the new Hobbit and mine from the "Problem of Pain."[5]

Each member of the group at one time or another praised another member for the quality of their writing. But like any good writing group, the Inkling's workshopped one another's writing harshly. Lewis's books were no exception. In his *Seeking the Secret Place*, Dorsett recalls the disdain Lewis's friends had for his work—"Indeed, J. R. R. Tolkien was embarrassed that *The Screwtape Letters* were dedicated to him."[6] Tolkien also said

2. Rogers, "Rejected by Oxford," 54.

3. Dorsett, *Seeking the Secret Place*, 58.

4. Diana Glyer's excellent *The Company They Keep* explores the Inklings' reciprocal communal influence upon one another, each member a "resonator," one who serves as a supportive, receptive soundboard, to the others' works. To study further the intellectual and fraternal support Lewis received for his writing, I really must recommend Glyer's entire book.

5. Hooper, *Collected Letters* 2.302.

6. Dorsett, *Seeking the Secret Place*, 58.

about Lewis's *The Great Divorce*: "I did not think so well of the concluding chapter of C. S. L's new moral allegory or 'vision' . . . ."[7]

Those that think Lewis enjoyed the unanimous support of his writing peers miss an important part of the triumph in his writing career. Where others might have put down the pen due to discouragement, Lewis wrote with a resolve without which we'd have no *The Problem of Pain, Great Divorce*, or *The Lion, the Witch and the Wardrobe*.

> I hear you you've been reading Jack's children's story. It really won't do, you know! I mean to say: "Nymphs and their Ways, The Love Life of a Faun." Doesn't he know what he's talking about?[8]

Lewis was beyond discouraged to know that his good friend Tolkien thought so poorly of his book. Biographer George Sayer captured how Tolkien's criticism hurt Lewis:

> Jack had always been constructively helpful and sympathetic with Tolkien's writing, and he probably expected similar treatment. He was hurt, astonished, and discouraged when Tolkien said that he thought the book was almost worthless.[9]

It wasn't the writing that Tolkien most disliked—though he did think the book "carelessly and superficially written"—but the product of Lewis's imagination. That Lewis would throw the likes of fauns, the White Witch, and Father Christmas in the same book, when they all had very different mythological origins. Tolkien never changed his mind and eventually gave up reading Lewis's Narnia novels. Sayer goes on in *Jack* to say,

> Jack had a high opinion of Tolkien's judgment and was distressed and by his harsh response, especially since he himself had little confidence in the merits of his story.[10]

If it weren't for the positive feedback from friend and eventual biographer Roger Green, Lewis would likely not have published the children's classic.

7. Tolkien, *Letters*, 71.

8. Green and Hooper, *C. S. Lewis: A Biography*, 241.

9. Sayer, *Jack*, 312.

10. Ibid., 313.

For the writer

It's amazing how delicate the writer can be. Looking to others for positive feedback and the encouragement to continue, writers worry over the process. Then, when the process is over, writers fret about the finished product, excited about who will like it and anxious over who won't. Just as amazing is how determined good writers are. Be it an unsupportive Oxford colleague, or, more likely, a discouraging friend, the writer must keep writing.

Do you feel supported in your writing? Is where you live helpful to your writing? Do your family and friends encourage—or criticize (or both)—your writing? As a writer, how important is support?

Do try: Write about your support system. A support system includes the place you live as well as those you experience life with. It's both Oxford and the Inklings. Write about yours. If you have one, write about your experience with and in it. If you don't, write about your writing life without it and why you might need it. Spend some time on this. Try to hit at least 500 words.

40

Like a Nightmare on My Chest

When I set out to write this book, I wanted to know how Lewis handled projects. I wanted to see how he worked through a book. I wanted to hear what he said about the writing process while he was going through it. I wanted to know how a writer so masterful and prolific in so many genres displayed his humanity when working on his craft, whether the writer whose work seemed to flow effortlessly from a fountainhead of genius ever struggled with a book. One discovery that meant as much to me as anything else I unearthed was Lewis's tenacity. Writing with a distinctly humble yet undeniably certain sense of self, Lewis was capable of writing with tenacious resolve, even with the books that gave him trouble.

We've seen Lewis's intermittent instinct to quit on a project that wasn't coming together. He never lost that. The author of *Mere Christianity*, *The Weight of Glory*, *The Allegory of Love*, and the seven Narnia novels was also the writer to tell Don Giovanni Calabria, "I am still working on my book on prayer: it was clearly not for me" before announcing two years later to Sister Penelope, "I have had to abandon the book on prayer."[1] But despite those times Lewis prudently put down the pen, his writing career testified to the power of creative, passionate resolve.

Lewis received his fair share of negative reviews—enough to make any writer question his vocation. They paper the backdrop of Lewis's remarkable life in letters, allowing us an accurate look at the personal and professional strife that came with his writing.

1. Hooper, *Collected Letters* 3.307, 428.

> As all reviews of *Perelandra* so far have been unfavourable or non-committal you will imagine with what pleasure I read your letter at breakfast. Say what you like, there's nothing like a true friend.[2]

By the time Lewis wrote that to Owen Barfield in 1943, he had already become famous. In 1940, Lewis published *The Problem of Pain*, which got the attention of James Welch, Director of Religious Broadcasting at the BBC and the man responsible for making C. S. Lewis's voice nationally known. Though *Perelandra* did receive its fair share of positive feedback, Lewis's growing popularity gave him no guarantee of positive reviews. In 1946, Lewis wrote to Sister Penelope, *"That Hideous Strength* has been unanimously damned by all reviewers."[3]

Lewis wasn't entirely correct, of course, as *That Hideous Strength* received its share of positive reviews. Fellow Christian writer Dorothy Sayers wrote Lewis on December 3, 1945, to say, "The book is tremendously full of good things."[4] But the negative reviews stuck with Lewis. They also matched what Lewis knew people thought of his work. At least one science-fiction fan suggested that Lewis might have been lynched had he shown up at one of their meetings.[5] Even Arthur C. Clarke, when he wrote to invite Lewis to speak at the British Interplanetary Society, warned, "It would be only fair to point out that your position might be somewhat analogous to that of a Christian martyr in the arena."[6]

Till We Have Faces, Lewis's most accomplished and sophisticated work, was also his most unpopular piece of writing at the time of publication. "It is my biggest failure yet," lamented Lewis.[7] It wasn't unusual for Lewis to feel unconfident in his work. After finishing *Letters to Malcolm Chiefly on Prayer*, Lewis said, "I've finished a book on Prayer. Don't know if it is any good."[8] Still, Lewis wrote.

Through abandoned books and disheartening reviews, Lewis, unfailingly driven to keep writing, pressed on. No book better shows Lewis's

---

2. Hooper, *Collected Letters* 2.574.

3. Ibid., 701.

4. Sayers, *Letters* 3.177.

5. Green and Hooper, *C. S. Lewis*, 177.

6. Quoted in Green and Hooper, *C. S. Lewis*, 177. Lewis declined Clarke's offer with quintessential humor and wit, "Probably the whole thing is only a plan for kidnapping me and marooning me on an asteroid! I know the sort of thing."

7. Hooper, *Collected Letters* 3.897.

8. Ibid., 1423.

writing resolve than the drawn out ordeal of *English Literature in the Six-teenth Century: Excluding Drama*. Lewis came to call *English Literature* "OHEL" because he wrote it as a contribution for the Oxford History of English Literature series. "OHEL" (o, hell) was apt. Lewis began the work 1935, didn't finish until 1952, and hated most every moment of writing it.

His process on this book was unorthodox. He would read a sixteenth-century author's work, almost immediately write an essay on the text, date it, stick it in a drawer with the rest for months, then pull them out and self-grade them. Any essays that Lewis didn't grade an A were rewritten. For such a formidably researched work of scholarship written in pieces over such a long period of time, there remains an accessibility and coherence to the book's structure.[9] The work was tedious.

OHEL reveals quite a lot about Lewis the writer. Lewis labored for over fifteen years on a book that didn't give Lewis any creative life. He spoke about writing it in fatigued tone. When Oxford granted him a yearlong sab-batical to finish the book, Lewis wrote, "I am plugging away at that as hard as I can."[10] Out of all Lewis's books, he felt the least confident in OHEL.

Lewis feared "hidden errors" in the book.[11] The kind that

> walks in silence till the day it turns irrevocable in a printed book
> and the book goes for review to the only man in England who
> w[oul]d have known it was a mistake.[12]

Lewis thought mistakes in his writing could mean lessons to his soul. If a bad bit of writing teaches the writer humility, then the mistakes would prove worth it:

> This, I suppose, is good for one's soul: and the kind of good I must
> learn to digest. I am going to be (if I live long enough) one of those
> men who was a famous writer in his forties and dies unknown—
> like Christian going own into the green valley of humiliation.[13]

To the editor of the OHEL series, Lewis declared:

---

9. In *The Narnian*, Alan Jacobs calls OHEL the "greatest of all of Lewis's books," not-ing especially its feel of "ease and charm" and witty tone; 183–84.

10. Hooper, *Collected Letters* 3.158.

11. Ibid., 149.

12. Ibid., 150.

13. Ibid.

> The O HELL lies like a nightmare on my chest ever since I got your specimen bibliography. . . . Do you think there's any chance of the world ending before the O HELL appears?[14]

He signed that letter, "yours, in deep depression . . ."[15]

Lewis preserved on the project until it, and he, were finished. Near the end of what felt like an eternal process, Lewis wrote,

> I'm busy at present finishing the heavy, academic work on 16th Century literature wh[ich] has occupied me (it has been the top tune—all the other books were only its little twiddly bits) for the last 15 years. When it is actually done I expect my whole moral character will collapse. I shall go up like a balloon that has chucked out the last sandbag.[16]

For the writer

Two things can cripple a writer more than anything: fear and discouragement. The opinions of others can be intimidating. Fear prevents writers from sending their work out, from daring to dream that they might be published. The threat of the bad review can hang over the writer, promising a very real possibility of embarrassment and shame. There is also the difficulty and discouragement of finishing a work. It's a true paradox that nothing can suck the life out of writing more than writing. But in both cases, there is nothing to be done for the writer except to keep plugging along. The successful writer is the stubborn writer, the tenacious writer with a passion for the craft and refusal to quit.

How do you handle discouragement? How do you handle unfavorable opinions of your work? What about insecurity that your work won't be any good? Do you continue writing? If not, why? What can you do to privilege the writing process during challenging times?

Do try: In at least 400 words, write about a time in your life when you've displayed tenacity. Focus on why you didn't quit, what you learned from preserving, and some of the challenges involved in staying with it.

---

14. Hooper, *Collected Letters* 2.222.
15. Ibid.
16. Ibid., 194.

41

An Absolute Corker

Lewis's growing popularity and eventuating fame had no adverse effect on his humility or congenial creativity. In his twenties, long before silent planets or savior lions, Lewis shared his writing with Greeves and Warnie. Sending his latest work, asking their opinion, dialoguing with their feedback, Lewis spent much of his creative energy in conversation. It's a testimony to Lewis's faith-born humility that he would become even more welcoming in his writing after seeing publishing success. An unseen conviction runs beneath Lewis's books, a view of and approach to creativity that Lewis never abandoned: writing is best done in relationship.

Lewis invited people into his writing, affirming them as thinkers and bolstering himself as a creator. In the early stages of writing *The Great Divorce*, Lewis shared his ideas with Dom Bede Griffiths, welcoming Griffiths's opinion:

> I wrote the other day "Good and evil when they attain their full stature are retrospective. That is why, at the end of all things, the damned will say we were *always* in Hell, and the blessed we have *never* lived anywhere but in heaven." Do you agree?[1]

"Do you agree?" stood as an important part of Lewis's writing process. Lewis eagerly engaged that process from both sides, as creator and critic. When Lewis read *The Missing Link* by Katharine Farrer, detective story writer, wife of philosopher and biblical scholar Austin Farrer, and one of

1. Hooper, *Collected Letters* 2.617.

Lewis's regular correspondents, he wrote, "About your dialogue I'm not so happy."[2] As specific as he was helpful in his criticism, Lewis continued,

> I think dialogue is frightfully tricky, partly because it is hard to stop writing it (characters *will* talk) and partly because so much that w[oul]d be alright in real conversation looks different when it gets into print.[3]

Lewis finished his letter by admitting that his advice, while helpful, was unsolicited: "But I don't know what right I have to talk like this, especially without being asked!"[4]

Mutually beneficial to both writers, these literary relationships usually lasted for years. Two years after *The Missing Link*, Lewis again wrote Katharine Farrer to comment on her novel, *The Cretan Counterfeit*, a book Lewis held in high regard. He offered Farrer praise—"I admire very much the thick-woven texture"[5]—and a range of suggestions for improvement:

> Would Clare have giggled? Or even if she had, isn't the word "giggled" too damaging?[6]

> I am outraged on p. 96 when you describe the moon "like the white face of an idiot lost in a wood." Dear lady, this is simply Eliotic.[7]

Eliotic, meaning like or characteristic of T. S. Eliot's writing, was far from a compliment. But Lewis labored to critique the work because he thought it worth critiquing, declaring "in general the actual writing is so good."[8] To his friends, Lewis remained a faithful fan, glowing over their work when it warranted praise. When he received poet Ruth Pitter's collection *The Ermine: Poems 1942–1952*, Lewis wrote, "I'm in a sea of glory!"[9] Lewis probably hadn't read all of the poems at that point, but he saw enough to know Pitter had hit upon something.

> This is just a line to be going on with, and to assure you at once that the new volume is an absolute Corker. . . . I wonder have you

2. Hooper, *Collected Letters* 3.97.
3. Ibid.
4. Ibid., 197.
5. Ibid., 423.
6. Ibid.
7. Ibid.
8. Ibid., 427.
9. Ibid., 327.

yourself any notion how good some of these are? But, as you see, I'm drunk on them at this present.[10]

Lewis rarely gave compliment with qualification. As with any good relationship, honesty underpinned Lewis's literary friendships. Of Roger Green's *King Arthur and the Knights of the Round Table*, Lewis assessed, "But far more important is your *K. Arthur*. I read every word and think you have done, *in general*, a v. good job."[11]

Lewis praised Green's style, particularly that his writing didn't feel modern. But he took issue with Green's overusing—or just using—needless adjectives:

> The style is exactly right: no unwelcome modernity, so that only close inspection reveals the absence of archaisms. The only place where you go wrong is on pp. 275–6 where you use the word *mysterious* four times. It wouldn't be a good adjective if used only once.[12]

Lewis sandwiched his criticism between two positive statements, ending his letter to Green with, "Despite this blot, it's a grand book: many, many thanks."[13]

To Sister Penelope, Lewis challenged, "In *style* I think you often fail of simplicity and concreteness," adding, "surely we ourselves didn't talk like that in 1940. One had got beyond vague metaphors . . . ."[14] Concerned with how antiquated her language sounded, Lewis pressed her to write in a more believable vernacular: "Unless you are going to write in archaic English throughout, I don't think any character sh[oul]d say 'Alas'. It is not living language at all."[15] And when acclaimed writer and friend Martyn Skinner sent Lewis a draft of *The Return of Arthur*, Lewis responded as feedback a "few details" in the form of over forty suggested line revisions.[16]

These creative exchanges defined Lewis's practice of and approach to writing. We never see Lewis outgrow them. His constant exchange with

---

10. Ibid., 327–28; Lewis followed up his initial letter to Ruth with another only a few days after. Though now "sober," Lewis held his first opinion of Pitter's works, Lewis wrote in praise and in greater detail of individual poems in the collection.

11. Ibid., 344. *Emphasis mine.*

12. Ibid.

13. Ibid.

14. Hooper, *Collected Letters* 2.590–91.

15. Ibid.

16. Ibid., 573.

other writers—both receiving and giving feedback—suggests the vital role relationships played in his writing, and writing in his relationships.

For the writer

A theme through this book has been the creative role relationships played in Lewis's writing. We've seen it again and again: for Lewis, writing included congenial, inviting, and challenging communication. Even more astonishing than Lewis's tireless tandem writing is that he never outgrew it. Lewis allowed neither fame nor his own expertise to hinder his habit of asking other opinions and giving his own. For the duration of his writing career, Lewis operated between "Do you agree?" and "It's an absolute corker!"

How has your writing benefited from the invitation and challenge of another's counsel? Can you think of specific points of advice you've received about your writing? What were they? Have you given specific points of advice on another's writing? What were they?

Do try: Twofold task: first, find someone you trust to send some of your latest writing to. Ask for positive and negative feedback. Once you've received their thoughts, respond with any questions or counters you have. Create a dialogue. Second, find someone who could trust you with their writing. Give positive and negative feedback. Invite them to ask questions and offer counters.

42

The Muscles of Language

As Lewis moved into the twilight of his writing life, he was asked more often to give his advice on writing. Scattered around in essays, interviews, and letters, we find advice from this great twentieth-century communicator. Lewis's advice ranged from the grammatical to the practical, touching on the writer's use of adverbs to the need for silence. With Lewis, we find an encompassing guide to the elements and style of writing.

Lewis advised novelist and journalist Jane Gaskell to

> never use adjectives or adverbs which are mere appeals to the reader to feel as you want him to feel. He won't do it just because you ask him: you've got to make him. No good telling us a battle was "exciting." If you succeeded in exciting us the adjective will be unnecessary: if you don't, it will be useless. Don't tell us the jewels had an "emotional" glitter; make us feel the emotion.[1]

This was Lewis's favorite piece of advice for writers. Virtually every writer Lewis corresponded with heard this at one time or another. Lewis thought this adjectival temptation led to inferior writing. To show instead of tell was paramount for the prose writer. As a rule, Lewis said, "I can hardly tell you how important this is."

At times, Lewis tailored his advice to the writer, anticipating the errors they might write themselves into. To one writer, after offering almost twenty points of specific correction, Lewis wrote,

---

1. Hooper, *Collected Letters* 3.881.

I hope this doesn't all sound too pedantic. But the matter is important. So many people, when they begin "research", lose all desire, and presently all power, of writing clear, sharp, and unambiguous English. Hold onto your finite transitive verb, your concrete nouns, and the *muscles* of language (*but, though, for, because* etc.). The more abstract the subject the more our language sh[oul]d avoid all unnecessary abstraction.[2]

Good writing is held up by what Lewis called "the muscles of language": finite verbs with clear subject and object, specific nouns, and sentence elements like functional conjunctions. Lewis suggests that the danger for the researcher is his loss of both desire and power to write clear English. If the writing is unclear, then the profundity of the idea won't matter.

Lewis's most explicit and lengthy prescription for good writing comes in response to a seventh-grade schoolgirl named Thomasine, who was assigned to write to her favorite author to ask his advice on writing. She, of course, chose Lewis. Lewis began his letter with, "It is very hard to give any general advice on writing," but proceeded to say,

(1) Turn off the Radio.

(2) Read all the good books you can, and avoid nearly all magazines.

(3) Always write (and read) with the ear, not the eye. You sh[oul]d hear every sentence you write as if it was being read aloud or spoken. If it does not sound nice, try again.

(4) Write about what really interests you, whether it is real things or imaginary things, and nothing else. (Notice this means that if you are interested *only* in writing you will never be a writer, because you will have nothing to write about.)

(5) Take great pains to be clear. Remember that though you start by knowing what you mean, the reader doesn't, and a single ill-chosen word may lead him to a total misunderstanding. In a story it is terribly easy just to forget that you have not told the reader something that he needs to know—the whole picture is so clear in your own mind that you forget that it isn't the same in his.

(6) When you give up a bit of work don't (unless it is hopelessly bad) throw it away. Put it in a drawer. It may come in useful later. Much

2. Ibid., 1069.

of my best work, or what I think my best, is the re-writing of things begun and abandoned years earlier.

(7) Don't use a typewriter. The noise will destroy your sense of rhythm, which still needs years of training.

(8) Be sure you know the meaning (or meanings) of every word you use.[3]

Create a silent space where you can concentrate, be filled to overflowing with ideas from books you've read, hear your language when you write by reading it aloud, write about something you're interested in, take pains to be clear, keep everything you work on (which Lewis was known not to do!), write by hand to build rhythm, and know the meaning of every word you use. Lewis's advice encompasses enough of the writing experience that any writer's work could stand to improve from heeding it.

Lewis had only so many points of advice to give, and if you read his essays, interviews, and letters long enough, you'll find he repeated himself. This is because the advice he gave was essential. When asked, "How would you suggest a young Christian writer go about developing a style?" Lewis answered in the same way he always had:

> The way for a person to develop a style is (a) to know exactly what he wants to say, and (b) to be sure he is saying exactly that. The reader, we must remember, does not start by knowing what we mean. If our words are ambiguous, our meaning will escape him. I sometimes think that writing is like driving sheep down a road. If there is any gate open to the left or the right the readers will most certainly go into it.

For the writer

Writers learn to write well by experience and by the advice of other writers. The craft can, indeed, be learned. Even the most talented writers learn their style from the counsel of other writers. The most gifted writing hints of those works that influenced it. Writers stand on the shoulders of other writers.

What advice has most helped you as a writer? Where did you get it? Another writer? A book? A teacher? What advice have you given others on the craft of writing?

3. Ibid., 1108.

Do try: Imagine that a beginning writer has asked your advice on how to improve his writing. What advice would you offer? Write a letter of advice to this beginning writer. Be specific, creative, and personal.

43

Use the Talent We Have

We find in Lewis's writing superb technique working from immense talent. So I'd be behindhand if, in a book on writing, I didn't give attention to talent. In his advice and the model of his life, Lewis wasn't one to give false hope to any would-be writer by neglecting to deal with the necessity of talent. Lewis once wrote back to a fan who inquired about the task of the Christian writer, "I think you have a mistaken idea of a Christian writer's duty. We must use the talent we have, not the talents we haven't."[1]

A writer, Christian or no, must have a talent for writing. Each writer works with what talents he has, and not the talents he doesn't. No two talents are the same, just as no two writers are the same. Each writer's talent is utterly his, not another's. This kind of creative individualism fits nicely into Lewis's larger theology. Lewis emphasized the importance of the individual's relationship to God, that every person must give to God the life he has, a truism he puts in the mouth of Aslan: "'Child,' said the Lion, 'I am telling you your story, not hers. No one is told any story but their own.'"[2]

Each his own talent. Each his own story. Each his own soul. For Lewis, the writer's talent isn't so unlike the human soul—both are utterly individual. In a particularly powerful moment in the chapter, "Heaven," in *The Problem of Pain*, Lewis wrote,

> The mold in which a key is made would be a strange thing, if you had never seen a key: and the key itself a strange thing if you had

1. Lewis, *Collected Letters* 3.502.
2. Lewis, *The Horse and His Boy*, 202.

never seen a lock. Your soul has a curious shape because it is a hollow made to fit a particular swelling in the infinite contours of the Divine substance, or a key to unlock one of the doors in the house with many mansions.[3]

The writer's talent is his. He has no other writer's, and no other writer can have his. The task of writing, then, is to know and work with what talent is given. The writer's talent is the strange key curiously shaped and fit only for the works he alone can write. And the Christian writer's individual talent fits a "particular swelling in the infinite contours" of God's will. What the writer's talent cannot be applied to is any piece of writing that celebrates the sinful: "We must *not* of course write anything that will flatter lust, pride or ambition."[4]

The misunderstanding Lewis suspects of this correspondent is that the Christian writer must write overtly Christian literature. Lewis believed that Christian writers should just write, letting the story dictate how evidently Christian it is. It could be that the less apparently Christian does more good:

> But we needn't all write patently moral or theological work. Indeed, work whose Christianity is latent may do quite as much good and may reach some whom the more obvious religious work would scare away.[5]

A story's "Christian-ness" is less important than it being a GOOD STORY—what Lewis calls a story's "first business."[6] "When Our Lord," Lewis wrote, "made a wheel in the carpenter shop, depend upon it: It was first and foremost a GOOD WHEEL."[7] There is no need to force specifically Christian themes into a creative work, as Lewis insisted: "if God wants you to serve him in that way, you will find it coming of its own accord."[8] And if God doesn't make it into the story, not to worry, "a good story which will give innocent pleasure is a good thing, just like cooking a good nourishing meal." Lewis ended the letter with what he considered "the great thing" for writers:

3. Lewis, *The Problem of Pain*, 152.

4. Lewis, *Collected Letters* 3.502.

5. Ibid.

6. Ibid.

7. Ibid. 502.

8. Ibid., 502–3.

to cultivate one's own garden, to do well the job which one's own natural capacities point out (after first doing well whatever the "duties of one's station" impose).[9]

In an interview he gave to *Decision* magazine the last year of his life, Lewis was asked, "If you had a young friend with some interest in writing on Christian subjects, how would you advise him to prepare himself?"[10] He answered,

> I would say if a man is going to write on chemistry, he learns chemistry. The same is true of Christianity. But to speak of the craft itself, I would not know how to advise a man how to write. It is a matter of talent and interest. I believe he must be strongly moved if he is to become a writer. Writing is like a "lust," or like "scratching when you itch." Writing comes as a result of a very strong impulse, and when it does come, I for one must get it out.[11]

It's interesting that Lewis says he wouldn't know how to advise a man to write. Given how often he gave practical advice, and since Lewis was nearing the end of his life when he gave the interview, it could be that Lewis thought the most important piece of advice he could give pertained to that intangible element in writing every bit as vital, if not more so, than the craft's practical points: talent.

For the writer

It takes good technique to write well. That's obvious. It also takes talent. Good writers are good writers because they have a knack for it. Call it a way with words, a love for language, keen artistic sensibilities, or a gift for telling stories, but talent is required. Interest, too, must exist. The writer's passion drives the entire endeavor. Thankfully, Lewis's journey as a writer, his successes and failures, and all of his advice to other writers imply that technique, talent, and even interest can develop. It's to that development the writer is called.

What do you think makes for talent in writing? How do you measure it? Being self-reflective of your own work, do you feel talented? What about interest—how would you describe your investment in writing?

9. Ibid.

10. Wirt, "Heaven, Earth, and Outer Space," 4.

11. Ibid.

Do try: Write about talent. What it is, if you can grow in it, and if you can, how it might be honed. Write about the role of talent in the act of writing. Be as creative, personal, or theoretical as you'd like to be.

44

It Is Like Bereavement in This Way

Lewis's ambition was to be a great poet. He had ordered the necessities of his life around his desire to write. *Spirits in Bondage* and *Dymer* were meant to establish Lewis's position as a respected writer. We know how the story goes. Lewis never became the poet he hoped to be. Instead, after converting to the Christian faith, he made himself known as a novelist, essayist, literary critic, apologist, and popular theologian.

In a note from 1948, poet Ruth Pitter asked herself why Lewis never broke through as a poet—"Did his great learning, & really staggering skill in verse inhibit the poetry?"[1]

Perhaps Lewis knew too much, was steeped in too much technique, was too fixated on perfect meter, his verse too allusive, his style too imitative.

> [It] is almost as though the adult disciplines, notably the technique of his verse, had largely inhibited his poetry, which is perhaps, after all, most evident in his prose.[2]

Both his brilliance and his life seemed to have perfectly suited him for poetry.

> He had a great stock of the makings of a poet: strong visual memory, strong recollections of childhood. . . . In fact his whole

---

1. Hooper, *Collected Letters* 2.882.
2. Ibid.

life was oriented & motivated by an almost uniquely-persisting child's sense of glory and of nightmare.[3]

Knowing Lewis's desire to be a poet and recognizing his inestimable significance as a writer in other genres, Pitter ended her note with, "I think he wanted to be a poet more than anything. Time will show. But if it was magic he was after, he achieved this sufficiently elsewhere."[4]

Pitter couldn't imagine how right she was. Lewis's indelible legacy to writing stretched farther than poetry would have allowed. We find the magic of Lewis's writing life in the ways he gave himself to it. The twentieth century hardly saw another writer so impassioned for, captivated by, and committed to enfleshing ideas through the written word.

Lewis lived his life in writing much the same exhaustive way he thought a work of art should be used. Lewis wrote to famed science fiction writer Arthur C. Clarke about the need to use every element in a work of literature:

> Surely in a work of art all the material should be used. If a theme is introduced into a symphony, something must be made of that theme. If a poem is written in a certain metre, the particular qualities of that metre must be exploited. If you write a historical novel, the period must be essential to the effect. For whatever in art is not doing good is doing harm . . . .[5]

Such was Lewis's approach to writing. All the material of his imagination, talent, and style used up writing that would long outlast him. His ability fully exploited for the craft. A Cair Paravel or Perelandra, a Screwtape or Cupid, all essential to his vision. Lewis used himself up on writing.

Lewis's life faded much the same way it was first illuminated, in hours spent writing and reading—"I write, read, and answer letters."[6] Lewis had a humble, even diminished, view of the lasting importance of his work. He believed that his writings would cease to sell after three years following his death, though Walter Hooper insisted that was not the case and that Lewis's readers were smart enough to know just how good his writing really was.[7] Lewis's humility wasn't the result of age. He started to speak about writing

---

3. Ibid.
4. Ibid.
5. Hooper, *Collected Letters* 3.412.
6. Ibid., 1481.
7. Ibid., 1457.

and himself with transparent meekness ever since becoming a Christian. Conversion loosened his grip on the ambition of his younger life. He was free to speak about the writing life with total unselfishness,

After his friend Harry Blamires published an unpopular, uncelebrated trilogy, Lewis wrote to comfort him, saying,

> I have had some experiences of such disappointments myself, first as an unpublished, and then as an unnoticed author. It is like bereavement in this way, that one's thoughts, long deeply engaged in one object, continue (20 times an hour) to set out on a familiar, and once delightful, road only to come up each time against the same roadblock. This sorrow is renewed and it is not one blow but a recurrent hammering. I find the only way is to treat it frankly as a pretty serious tribulation and deal with it, before God, as one w[oul]d deal with any other.[8]

Lewis remained a warm nurturing voice to other writers.[9] And he could speak with authority not just because he knew writing's disappointments but because he knew writing to be worth the disappointment. Lewis never treated writing ironically. For Lewis, writing was as serious as any other part of life, to be sacrificed for, prayed about, and taken to God with.

Writing remained a source of happiness for Lewis, and he was quick to name it as a comfort—along with the company of his friends.

> I'm afraid I'm condemned to an invalid life for the rest of my days . . . but when I look around me and see how much worse off many other people are, I am grateful for my condition. I am able to write, and my friends are very good about coming to see me.[10]

Though Lewis kept writing, managing to finish *A Grief Observed* and *An Experiment in Criticism* in the last years of his life, "his inspiration had dried up" and "he no longer saw pictures."[11] He stopped working on a book called *After Ten Years* as well as collaboration in progress with Roger Green titled *Wood that Time Forgot*.[12] At the end, one of the twentieth century's

---

8. Ibid., 682.

9. For example, to encourage a writer named Kathy Kristy, Lewis wrote, "I hope you will enjoy the Screwtape Letters which has been the most popular of all my books. I sympathize with your 'maddening experience,' but I can assure you that this is one of the occupational risks of authorship . . ."; Ibid., 1479.

10. Ibid., 1479.

11. Green and Hooper, *C. S. Lewis*, 297.

12. About the "Wood that Time Forgot," Lewis wrote, "The two alternatives that float

greatest sources of imagination and literary accomplishment had become, as Lewis designated himself, an "extinct volcano."[13]

For the writer

Perhaps, the greatest legacy a writer can leave is a life faithful to the practice of writing. Beyond publication, fame, or accolades, the great writers have written for writing's sake. The years spent devoted to the craft—through years of disappointment, achievement, self-doubt, and hope—is the writer's greatest work. That all writers would spend themselves on the writing life, eventually—after years of eruptive imagination and prolific output—ending their careers, like Lewis, as extinct volcanoes.

What would make for a successful writing life? What kind of writer do you want to be? What do you want to be known for? How do you want to be remembered as a writer?

Do try: In 750–1,000 words, write about the creative vision you have for your life. Write about your dreams. Write about the kind of work you want to give yourself to. Write about how you want to be remembered as a writer. Dream big, write boldly.

---

before my mind are these: A. Re-write as a straight romance about people living no one knows where or when and cut out the children altogether. B. Re-write as a novel told in the first person. . ."; Green and Hooper, *C. S. Lewis*, 297.

13. Ibid., 1449.

45

Of Loathing and Letter Writing

No book titled *C. S. Lewis and the Art of Writing* could be so called if it did not say something of the letter writing to which Lewis devoted so much time. Over his lifetime, Lewis penned thousands of letters, and hated writing most every one of them. Lewis's letters constitute an entire body of writing separate from his published works, providing us with a comprehensive, honest look into Lewis's life. They span almost sixty years, include correspondence with those personally and professionally closest to Lewis, give us rare glimpses into some of Lewis's views about certain writers and types of writing, and open outlooks to his creative development. It's interesting, then, that these texts—so valuable and revealing to us readers—were so often begrudgingly written by Lewis.

As with his fictive and poetic juvenilia, Lewis started to write letters very early in life. A young boy sympathetic to the decorum of daily correspondence, Lewis gave hours to writing letters:

> You must excuse me writing a long letter as I have a lot of people to write.[1]
> And now as the time allotted for correspondence is drawing to a close, etc.[2]
>
> I have written from 10 to quarter past 11 . . .[3]

1. Hooper, *Collected Letters* 1.7.
2. Ibid., 12.
3. Ibid., 191.

We get a sense of how little Lewis enjoyed writing letters when, in recalling his day-to-day life with tutor W. T. Kirkpatrick at Bookham, he wrote,

> But when is a man to write his letters? You forget that I am describing the happy life I led with Kirk or the ideal life I would live now if I could. And it is essential of the happy life that a man would have almost no mail and never dread the postman's knock.[4]

Lewis would spend hours upon days upon months dreading the postman's knock, knowing that each letter meant he'd have to answer

> earnest questioners, lonely hearts, and megalomaniacs whose pleas the Royal Mail delivered so consistently to his door, day after day, season succeeding season, world without end, Amen.[5]

Lewis, the "last great letter-writer," simply loathed it.[6] But, loathed as the letters were, Lewis did, on rare occasion, recognize their value. At the beginning of a touching letter in the summer of 1930, a reflective Lewis wrote to Greeves, his dearest lifelong epistolary companion,

> Thank you for writing—I enjoyed your two letters enormously. Do stop apologizing for them and wondering archly . . . how I can read them. Surely it needs no great imagination for you to realize that every mention of things at home now comes to me with the sweetness that belongs only to what is irrevocable. Secondly, there are a great many subjects on which you are the only person who I can write to or be written to by with full understanding.[7]

Letters allowed Lewis to yearn for—and in a way revisit—home, that place where he first met *Sehnsucht*. As his years of correspondence with Greeves so beautifully exhibit, letter writing became the lifeblood of the relationships that meant the most to him. But even with those he was unacquainted who so regularly wrote him, Lewis handled each letter with great care and personal interest. Joan Lancaster, the once young girl whose letter inspired this book, exchanged letters with Lewis for almost ten years. In a 1962 letter to Lancaster, Lewis made mention of his index of letters, which

---

4. Lewis, *Surprised by Joy*, 143.

5. Jacobs, *The Narnian*, 226.

6. Hooper, "Preface," *Collected Letters* 3.XV; cf. *Collected Letters* 3.1464.

7. Hooper, *Collected Letters* 1.916.

recorded to whom and for how long he had corresponded. In December of 1962, Lewis wrote to Lancaster,

> We have been corresponding since 1954 . . . Attached to your card
> is a photo of yourself in those days, and no doubt you look very
> different now. You have one consolation which I have not; for you,
> from now onwards and for many years, times will get better and
> better.[8]

Lewis—here quite personable, sentimental, and merry—goes on to joke about which of her high school courses he would shudder to think of taking. Unfortunately, not every sender was so affable, and for the most part, Lewis didn't enjoy spending his time responding to people with whom he had no desire to converse: "And now for piles of Christmas letters: many of them, unlike yours, from people I don't want to write to at all."[9]

Even in 1963, the last year of his life—a time when Lewis would regularly spend two hours after breakfast answering mail despite the rheumatism that pained his hands to the point of paralysis—Lewis devoted his energy to suffering the insufferable. To a provocative Father Peter Milward, who had wrongly attributed Lewis's fiction to the influence of several authors, Lewis once replied,

> Trying to goad a man into controversy when he has declined it is
> not the way to convert him. Leave that to the Tee-Totallers and
> Pacifists who honour me with frequent letters. . . . It is not likely
> I sh[oul]d prefer the manual labour (half my life spent answering
> letters anyway) of a vast correspondence with a man at the other
> end of the world.[10]

Half a life spent answering letters to Milwards, tee-totallers, and pacifists was hardly what Lewis had in mind as a man of letters. But he was faithful in writing, nonetheless, even when there were "infinite other letters to answer."[11]

It is ironic, given how they plagued him, that the countless hours Lewis spent writing letters were his most extensive, consistent form of writing practice. Undeniably, letter writing provided Lewis with a kind of daily literacy that allowed him to practice his craft. In Lewis's letters we meet

8. Hooper, *Collected Letters* 3.1399.

9. Ibid., 396.

10. Ibid., 1433.

11. Ibid., 295.

the exact kind of logical thinking, conversational style, clear language, and immense capacity to process through complex thought that most define works like *Mere Christianity*, *The Screwtape Letters*, *The Great Divorce*, and *The Problem of Pain*. It's hard to imagine a writer more versed in the facets and phases of the craft, and harder to imagine that the sheer practice of writing letters did not improve his capacity in that craft. Loathed as they were, letters gave Lewis practice. They helped shape his style and form his voice.

For the writer

Despite the lure of publication or any dream of exposure, what matters most to the writer—what most exercises his talent and deepens his instincts—could be the writing no one was ever meant to see. As Lewis once told Greeves, to be a better writer he needed to practice, practice, practice. Nothing afforded Lewis more practice than writing letters. Any writing that gives the writer time to find her voice, work on paragraph structure, refine sentences, or practice melody in phrases is formative. Chances to write—mundane, unglorified, and resented as they may be—situate the writer exactly where she needs to be, in her craft.

What writing practice does life regularly give you? How could you turn daily literacy—correspondence of any kind that requires you to use written language—into craft practice?

Do try: Think of the writing you've done in the last couple of weeks. Choose any one thing you've written—something normal or commonplace—and turn it into a creative piece: essay, short story, poem, play. Be inventive. Transform the quotidian into the creative.

46

Make Quite Clear What You Mean

When Lewis answered young Joan Lancaster's question about makes for good writing, he started his five-point reply with,

> Always try to use the language so as to make quite clear what you mean and make sure your sentence couldn't mean anything else.[1]

By the time Lewis wrote to young Joan Lancaster in 1955, the majority of his published writing lay behind him. By 1955, Lewis had been writing for fifty years. His advice on writing was born of vast experience. Of Lewis's five points of advice, all of which perfectly describe his own prose, perhaps he best epitomized this first rule on clarity. "Quite clear" banners his every book, exemplifying every essay. As a writer's writer, Lewis gives a prescription for all who would take up the pen: at the level of word and sentence, write with unmistakable clarity through crystalline language.

Lewis had a renowned ability to make clear what he meant. Nevill Coghill, with whom Lewis exchanged quite a lot of letters, a few we've already seen, said of Lewis's writing,

> The marks of his style are weight and clarity of argument, sudden turns of generalization and genial paradox, the telling short sentence to sum a complex paragraph, and unexpected touches of personal approach to the reader, whom he always assumes to

---

1. Hooper, *Collected Letters* 3.766.

be as logical, as learned, as romantic, and as open to conviction as himself.[2]

We don't have to read long to see what Coghill means. Lewis handled the most complex issues the same way he handled the simple, with encapsulating efficiency and obvious, accessible language. Because of his commitment to clarity, intrinsically complex ideas so often seem simple. In his essay, "The Efficacy of Prayer," Lewis approaches the potentially difficult task of exploring the essence of prayer by parsing the idea of request and compulsion:

> Now even if all the things that people prayed for happened, which they do not, this would not prove what Christians mean by the efficacy of prayer. For prayer is request. The essence of request, as distinct from compulsion, is that it may or may not be granted.[3]

Writers might miss such an obvious way to describe petition in prayer because they think it too simple, not academic enough. But Lewis understood that complexity should be relegated to ideas, and clarity to the explanation of those ideas.

Lewis's *Studies in Words* serves as a grander example of his admonition, "make quite clear what you mean." The book is a love letter to language, a product of Lewis's long-lived practice of studying the exact meaning of a word, along with the word's full semantic range. There are two levels of clarity in *Studies in Words*. First, there is Lewis's philosophical belief that language must be clear, which lies behind the book's most important points. For the craft of writing, Lewis's assumption in *Studies in Words* proves important: precise words make for powerful writing. Lewis begins his philological project with a reminder that a study of literature free from a "love and knowledge of words" is either a "crying for the moon or else resolving on a lifetime of persistent and carefully guarded delusion."[4] Finding the meaning of a word, the exact connotation the author intended, is the reader's responsibility just as using the right word is the author's. Wise readers don't just want the sense of a word, but rather "to find the sense the author intended."[5]

---

2. Coghill, "The Approach to English," 60.
3. Lewis, "The Efficacy of Prayer," 4.
4. Lewis, *Studies in Words*, 3.
5. Ibid., 5.

Writers would do well to remember that Lewis's scrutiny of the right usage of the right word implies what he confesses to be an idea of what is good and bad language. The kind of prolonged thought about words Lewis embarks on can create reticence in those whose ordinary use of words is less exhaustive. But such strenuous thinking about language is a prerequisite for good writing. The best language, Lewis says, "can with the greatest ease make the finest and most numerous distinctions of meaning."[6] Modern writing, Lewis contends, has spawned a vast verbicide, word murder, resulting in inflated and evaluative, rather than concrete and plain, language.

Conflating a word's meaning from one sense to another—for example, "psychology," can mean the name of a science as well as that which the science studies—serves one of Lewis's chief points in the book: that given language's changing nature, its ever-morphing history, that words require a crystalline touch.

The second level of clarity in *Studies in Words* is the example of Lewis's writing in it. Though the philology can be challenging and Lewis's references unfamiliar, the syntax in *Studies in Words* remains unequivocal:

> Unless we are writing a dictionary, or a text-book of some technical subject, we define our words only because we are in some measure departing from their real current sense.[7]

> A man's woruld [world], as we have seen, can be his life. And worulda in the plural can be ages. By keeping these two shades of meaning together in our minds we shall best understand the sense I now have to investigate.[8]

> Language exists to communicate whatever it can communicate. Some things it communicates so badly that we never attempt to communicate them by words if any other medium is available.[9]

In *Studies of Words*, we see a writer whose love for language enlivens his writing and one whose writing best tokens his love of language. It's as Austin Farrer, philosopher, theologian, and friend, said of Lewis's prose: "muddled minds read him, and found themselves moving with delight in a world of clarity."[10] Often, Lewis ensured clarity by explicitly stating when

6. Ibid., 6.

7. Ibid., 18.

8. Ibid., 217.

9. Ibid., 313.

10. Farrer, "The Christian Apologist," 29.

he was trying to be clear. In his essay, "On Living in an Atomic Age," Lewis addresses the reader with, "This brings us much nearer to the real point; but let me try to make clear exactly what I think that point is."[11]

In this same essay, Lewis enumerates his main ideas, "this is the first point to be made" and "it is, then, on the second question that we really need to make up our minds" and "in this situation there are, I think, three things one might do."[12] This might seem like a heavy-handed move, but Lewis was more interested in clarity than risking cloaking what he meant. To Lewis, nothing excused opaque writing. And he was disappointedly astonished at how badly a certain world-famous professional colleague put together even the simplest sentence—a sign, he thought, of a fundamental insensitivity to language."[13]

Now, when we turn to his fiction, we witness Lewis's first rule of writing—"make quite clear what you mean"—creatively incarnated. Lewis seems to have grasped this rule of clarity very early in life. His early writing in *Boxen* might be prosaic, but its prose is rather clear.

> In case our readers have not guessed it, it may be expedient to state that our young feline was a naval marine officer, who, having been just recently freed from the trammels of a naval college, was on his way to join his first vessel.[14]

When Lewis began *The Last Battle* with, "In the last days of Narnia, far up to the west beyond Lantern Waste and close beside the great waterfall, there lived an Ape,"[15] he gave readers one last passage into Narnia through a perfectly clear door. A reader could know nothing else about the Chronicles yet understand in this single sentence all that's necessary to enter the novel's plot. Lewis gives us setting, character, and most importantly, clear prose. The book's end—with its closing encounter between the Pevensie children and Aslan, Narnia's Christ-lion—is every bit as brilliantly clear as its beginning.

> And as He spoke He no longer looked to them like a lion; but the things that began to happen after that were so great and beautiful that I cannot write them. And for us this is the end of all the stories,

11. Lewis, "On Living in an Atomic Age," 74.

12. Ibid., 74–76.

13. Raine, "From a Poet," 103.

14. Lewis, *Boxen*, 154.

15. Lewis, *The Last Battle*, 3.

and we can most truly say that they all lived happily ever after. But for them it was only the beginning of the real story. All their life in this world and all their adventures in Narnia had only been the cover and the title page: now at last they were beginning Chapter One of the Great Story which no one on earth has read: which goes on forever: in which every chapter is better than the one before.[16]

For the writer

Clarity is writing's cardinal virtue. If the writing isn't quite clear, and the reader can't understand what the writer is trying to communicate, then its very reason for being is nullified. The good writer runs every sentence by "is this absolutely clear?" Every paragraph, the work in its entirety, must submit to the same clarion standard. If a word, phrase, or sentence can mean anything other than what the author specifically intends, then further revision for clarity is needed.

At the levels of grammar, word choice, and syntax, what exactly makes a sentence *quite clear*? What tendencies do you have that might diminish your writing's clarity? Lewis advises to "use the language" that will make for the clearest sentence: how can you revise your language to prevent it from being misunderstood?

Do try: Lewis wrote clearly by mastering a few techniques. One of those techniques was explaining an idea through distinctly marked points of evidence or explanation. He also used analogies to clarify complex ideas. Choose a theme or pressing issue—it can be anything, just think complex or abstract—and in 300 words, write about that theme incorporating a *list of evidence for your position* as well as an *analogy* to help explain your thinking.

16. Ibid., 211.

47

Prefer The Plain

This is the second rule Lewis gave Joan Lancaster,

> Always prefer the plain direct word to the long, vague one. Don't implement promises, but keep them.[1]

Now when Lewis tells Lancaster to "prefer the plain," he speaks of writing's accessibility, its exactness. Throughout his prose, both fiction and nonfiction, Lewis aims at unadorned, austere language. Lewis's diction is lucid. Verbal plainness in Lewis's writing is not synonymous with limited word choice, nor is it due to a lack of appreciation for beautiful language. His sentences, while beautiful, cut through ambiguity.

The Pilgrim's Regress, Lewis's first venture into fiction after becoming a Christian, models plainness in prose. We'll recall just how *Regress* presents a paradox in process. A lesson to writers—albeit often not imitable—to push on when inspiration and opportunity allow, Lewis wrote *Pilgrim's Regress* in just two weeks. Two weeks to write an impressively creative and personal portrayal of Lewis's journey into Christian belief. On the other hand, it is clear that Lewis wrote the novel too hastily. His apology in the afterword to the third edition for the novel's "chief faults"—its "needless obscurity, and an uncharitable temper"—reveal Lewis to be a mere mortal, after all.[2]

Regardless of how quickly Lewis wrote *Pilgrim's Regress*, the novel bears Lewis's signature univocal voice, apparent style, and verbal plainness.

---

1. Hooper, *Collected Letters* 3.66.
2. See David Downing's excellent annotated edition, p. 207.

While at times hopelessly allusive with its often unannounced references to Virgil, Dante, Donne, and Kant, *Regress* is a premier example of plain prose through simple diction. Lewis begins with childlike language and with all the conventions of a well-worn folktale, "I dreamed of a boy who was born in the land of Puritania and his name was John."[3] The first person narrator, simple passive voice verbs, and practical syntax announce a familiar form of storytelling as well as a particular philosophy of functional language.

> . . . and I dreamed that when John was able to walk he ran out of his parents' garden on a fine morning on to the road. And on the other side of the road there was a deep wood.

Pilgrim Regress opens up through significant, though not tedious, details. The story of *Pilgrim's Regress*, built on the simple phrases "when John was able to walk" and "garden on a fine morning" and "there was a deep wood," is quite plain.

The novel's first bit of dialogue invites the reader into a world of characters who share their narrator's view of language:

> "Why?" said John. "Because the Steward would be very angry," said cook. "Who is the Steward?" said John. "He is the man who makes rules for all the country round here," said cook. "Why?" said John. "Because the Landlord set him to do it." "Who is the Landlord?" said John. "He owns all the country," said the cook.[4]

As in Bunyan's *Progress*, Lewis's allegorical inspiration, we're led by a trustworthy narrator. He narrates with transparent diction.

> But you want to hear about Savage. He sat on a high chair at the end of his barn—a very big man, almost a giant. When I say that I don't mean his height: I had the same feeling about him that I had about the dwarfs. That doubt about the species. He was dressed in skins and had an iron helmet on his head with horns stuck in it.[5]

The narrator is unpretentious. His description, plain.

> All their journey South had been a descent, from the northern mountains to Mr. Sensible's: but after his house it began to rise again a little to the main road, which ran along a low ridge, so

---

3. Lewis, *The Pilgrim's Regress*, 7.
4. Ibid., 7.
5. Ibid., 104.

that, when they had gained the road, the country South of it was suddenly all opened before them.[6]

The importance of Lewis's plain prose lies in his belief that good writing should hit its mark. It must be understood. At the level of language, good writing meets readers where they are. Lewis speaks to this principle in an essay called "Christian Apologetics":

> You must translate every bit of your Theology into the vernacular. This is very troublesome, and it means you say very little in half an hour, but it is essential. It is also of the greatest service to your own thought. I have come to the conviction that if you cannot translate your thoughts into uneducated language, then your thoughts were confused. Power to translate is the test of having really understood one's own meaning.[7]

Uneducated language—far from being ignorant or uninformed language—is unadorned language. Lewis means language that reflects a sound comprehension of the ideas one means to communicate. Lewis's apologetic writing masterfully models this vernacular control. In every high theological concept he aimed to communicate, Lewis employed a quotidian analogy, a mundane metaphor, a simple simile, a plain term, thereby empowering "muddled minds" to find themselves "moving with delight in a world of clarity."[8] The theologian's job is similar to the writer's: say the powerful, but plainly. It's no good addressing theodicy—why evil exits if God is good and all-powerful—if you can't articulate it memorably through plain presentation:

> A man can no more diminish God's glory by refusing to worship Him than a lunatic can put out the sun by scribbling the word "darkness" on the walls of his cell.[9]

> God whispers to us in our pleasures, speaks in our conscience, but shouts in our pain: it is His megaphone to rouse a deaf world.[10]

---

6. Ibid., 114.

7. Lewis, "Christian Apologetics," 98.

8. From Austin Farrer's description of Lewis's affect on readers: "Muddled minds read him, and found themselves moving with delight in a world of clarity"; "The Christian Apologist," 29.

9. Lewis, *The Problem of Pain*, 46.

10. Ibid., 91.

Perhaps Lewis's most austere example of preferring the plain is the sharp sorrows of *A Grief Observed*. This is Lewis's most honest book. In it he pours himself out in grief over his wife Joy's death, questioning the God who allows such severe pain with the plain speech of everyman.

> I have no photograph of her that's any good. I cannot even see her face distinctly in my imagination. Yet the odd face of some stranger seen in a crowd this morning may come before me in vivid perfection the moment I close my eyes tonight.[11]

Lewis's prose was never so powerful. The pathos behind his writing can only come through because the writing itself is so unveiled.

> Talk to me about the truth of religion and I'll listen gladly. Talk to me about the duty of religion and I'll listen submissively. But don't come talking to me about the consolations of religion or I shall suspect that you don't understand.[12]

The language is living, full of known references and common imagery.[13] Lewis wanted to capture the severity of his grief, to say the religiously unsayable in the most human of ways.

> What do people mean when they say, "I am not afraid of God because I know He is good"? Have they never even been to a dentist?[14]

> When I lay these questions before God I get no answer. But a rather special sort of "No answer." It is not the locked door. It is more like a silent, certainly not uncompassionate, gaze.[15]

For the writer

Plainness seems an obvious quality of good writing, yet so many writers fail to rein in their writing to its most accessible state. For all his brilliance, despite his undeniable ability to write as abstractly as he desired, Lewis committed his writing to sentences like, "This last point needs a little plain

11. Lewis, *A Grief Observed*, 15.

12. Ibid., 25.

13. "The ideal of 'timeless English' is sheer nonsense. No living language can be timeless. You might as well ask for a motionless river." Lewis, *Letters to Malcolm*, 6.

14. Lewis, *A Grief Observed*, 43.

15. Ibid., 69.

speaking," when explaining a potentially tricky point on the subject of gender equality;[16] "David, we know, danced before the Ark";[17] and "The confusion was dreadful."[18] The good writer knows that the goal of writing is the reader's comprehension, not the writer's ostentation.

Is writing plainly a challenge for you? If so, why? If not, why do you think it is such a common problem with writers? What beliefs about writing must you first have to "prefer the plain"? What beliefs about writing might be at work with those authors who prefer to "implement" promises, rather than "keep" them?

Do try: Think of an important moment in your life. It could be a particularly painful moment or memorably joyous time. Spend one hour writing about that moment with a commitment to plain prose. No matter how complicated or personal the moment, write it with an everyman readership in mind. Proof your writing by reading each sentence aloud, asking yourself if your writing is understandable, and your meaning, evident.

16. Lewis, "Equality," 19.

17. Lewis, *Reflections on the Psalms*, 45.

18. Lewis, *Boxen*, 38.

48

Concrete Ones Will Do

Make quite clear what you mean, prefer the plain, and then, Lewis wrote to Lancaster, "Never use abstract nouns when concrete ones will do. If you mean 'More people died' don't say 'Mortality rose.'"[1]

One of Lewis's gifts to writing lies here. Avoiding abstraction, composing with the concrete, and writing with the weight of solidly lucid diction and syntax defined Lewis's craft. In his fiction and nonfiction, Lewis labored under this rule. Whether in literary essay, apologetic work, or fantasy story, Lewis had the ability to hit upon the concrete word. His phrases had a particularity about them. When he wrote about a thing, he did so with immediacy. He dealt in specifics. "When concrete ones will do" issues a call to writers to go with the common but clear rather than the ornate but opaque.

Examples of this rule are everywhere in Lewis's writing—sentences direct and hard as nails, like: "There is a Pagan, savage heart in me somewhere."[2]

To Lewis, "concrete ones will do" wasn't only a dictum. Lewis also runs the theme of concrete language through his work. In *The Great Divorce*, Lewis contrasts the solid reality of the redeemed with the translucent, ghostly reality of the unredeemed. In his theological fiction, Lewis sees heavenly reality as being dense, weighed down by its own ultimate reality. Concretely real in every way. When the unredeemed ghosts first step onto the heavenly high green plains, their unreality can't bear it. Their feet aren't

1. Hooper, *Collected Letters* 3.766.
2. Lewis, *Reflection on the Psalms*, 98.

hard enough. They aren't substantial enough to live in that world. And their speech reflects their mealy existence. The ghosts' words are abstract, vague, as George MacDonald, the narrator's heavenly guide, described:

> In the actual language of the Lost, the words will be different, no doubt. One will say he has always served his country right or wrong; and another that he has sacrificed everything to his Art; and some that they've never been taken in, and some that, thank God, they've always looked after Number One, and nearly all, that, at least they've been true to themselves.[3]

These are opaque phrases. Vague, unclear, and ultimately meaningless. Lewis contrasts the ghosts' abstruse language with the "solid" people's concrete speech. The narrator, who is Lewis, asks MacDonald, "Then those people are right who say that Heaven and Hell are only states of mind?" MacDonald replies, "Do not blaspheme. Hell is a state of mind—ye never said a truer word. But Heaven is not a state of mind. Heaven is reality itself."[4] Reality and concreteness are synonymous. Lewis said in "Myth Became Fact" that "[h]uman intellect is incurably abstract" while asserting that "the only realities we experience are concrete."[5] Lewis works with this notion in *The Great Divorce*, giving his most real characters the most concrete language, going as far as associating that language with moral weight. They speak most concretely because they are redeemed.

The most concrete of nouns in the novel is "God." In one particular exchange, a ghostly famous artist finds himself meandering about the great green country, exclaiming, "God." A solid spirit overhears the ghost's "God" and asks, "God what?" Uncomprehending, the ghost replies, "What do you mean, 'God what'?" To which the spirit answers, "In our grammar God is a noun." The ghost is left to ambiguous speech, an inexact, erroneous language. "Oh—I see. I only meant 'By Gum' or something of the sort."[6] The ghost stumbles his speech in search for the right noun to describe the high heavenly countries, "well, all this. It's . . . it's . . . I should like to paint this." The spirit informs the ghost that trying to capture ultimate reality through a medium like painting when actually standing in that reality quite misses the point. The spirit's lesson is that, in life and in words, one should choose the concrete.

3. Lewis, *The Great Divorce*, 70.

4. Ibid., 70.

5. Lewis, "Myth Became Fact," 65–66.

6. Lewis, *Great Divorce*, 83.

Lewis's belief that the "concrete one will do" is also behind his writing style in *Mere Christianity*. Originally delivered over the BBC during World War II, Lewis had to read the lectures that would comprise *Mere Christianity* within a specific time frame, usually no longer than fifteen minutes. To fill that short time slot with powerfully rich writing on transcendent beliefs requires specific language. So in *Mere Christianity*, when Lewis writes about the moral ideas of the just and unjust, he concretely repeats the terms "just" and "unjust" and specifies the argument for which the terms are used.

> My argument against God was that the universe seemed so cruel and unjust. But how had I got this idea of just and unjust? A man does not call a line crooked unless he has some idea of a straight line. What was I comparing this universe with when I called it unjust? If the whole show was bad and senseless from A to Z, so to speak, why did I, who was supposed to be part of the show, find myself in such violent reaction against it? A man feels wet when he falls into water, because man is not a water animal: a fish would not feel wet.[7]

Just and unjust. A to Z. The analogy of falling into water. These are Lewis's first, simple ways of concretizing his diction. Concrete composition requires clarity of mind as well as a commitment to definite nouns and verbs. It is an ideology. The writer strives for concreteness because the ideas that make up his life and language are worthy of exact expression. Lewis's poetry bore this mark, as well:

> Durned and dwindled. Dwarflike he seemed,
> But his ears bigger than any other man's.
> He was grubby as if he had grown from the ground, plantlike,
> Big of belly, and with bandy legs.
> Shrublike his shape, shocked-headed too,[8]

Lewis insisted that the good writer must say exactly what he wants to say, "you must know what you want to say and say exactly that."[9] The writer uses a vocabulary of certainty. Each phrase from a skilled writer should drip with concrete reality.

---

7. Lewis, *Mere Christianity*, 38.
8. Lewis, "The Nameless Isle," 115.
9. Lewis, "Cross-Examination," 263.

For the writer

Concrete language is grounded language. Writers face the temptation to write in flowery prose. Some writers might think that ornate, verbose prose makes for good writing. Simple phrases are disdained and deemed elementary. Lewis's writing contends the contrary. While Lewis, whose love for poetry and romance lasted his entire life, was quite capable of gilded prose and opulent sentence construction, his commitment was to clear, effective communication. If Lewis's style suggests anything, it's that lofty topics should never compromise concrete prose.

What verbal elements make for concrete prose? Considering your current writing style at the level of word choice, short phrase, and sentence construction, how can you begin to write more concretely?

Do try: Select something you've already written, and go back through to revise it, looking for words that you can revise to make more concrete. Take notes on what you learn about yourself as a writer and how challenging it can be to write concretely.

49

Instead of Telling Us a Thing . . . Describe It

The fourth rule Lewis gave Joan Lancaster was:

> Don't use adjectives which merely tell us how you want us to feel
> about the thing you are describing. I mean, instead of telling us a
> thing was "terrible," describe it so that we'll be terrified.[1]

Lewis encouraged what might be called the literary novelist's modus
operandi—"show me, don't tell me." As mentioned, Lewis advised others
on this exact point. Experienced, talented writers tended to fall into the
same "tell us" trap, and Lewis tended to slap their writing hand for it. Lewis
corrected Roger Green on this same issue:

> I forget whether I have said before—and anyway I am going to
> say *now*—that adjectives which are direct command to the reader
> to feel a certain emotion are no use. In vain do we *tell* him that a
> thing was horrible, beautiful, or mysterious. We must present it so
> that *he* exclaims horrible! beautiful! or mysterious![2]

As well as Sister Penelope:

> On Style. You have already erased euologistic adjectives . . .
> go through now and erase the rest or replace them with real
> descriptive adjectives. Near the bottom of p. 2 is an example—the
> sentence "except for . . . superb." It's no good telling us that things
> were "lovely," "exquisite," and "superb. We won't believe you. You

1. Hooper, *Collected Letters* 3.766.
2. Ibid., 344.

221

must describe them so that we say "lovely" etc. Instead of "lovely" for shadows I want an adjective telling me about their colour, or texture, or size, or shape, or motion . . . etc.[3]

Lewis believed that good writing painted a world for—rather than prescribed it to—the reader. Inarguably, the best prose creates a vivid world through descriptive sensory language. Lewis knew this early. Of all Lewis's creative instincts and innate talents, descriptive writing seems to be the one he developed earliest. As early as *Boxen*, Lewis could "describe it":

> The pitiless glare of the sun beat down on the angular bazaar-street of the wine-sellers, so brilliantly that it hurt Lord Big's eyes to look at the white alabaster walls of the houses: that the clearly defined shadows appeared as black as jet: a confused babel of shrill discordant voices filled the leaden atmosphere.[4]

Even in his personal correspondence Lewis had a penchant for poignant sensory language. In a letter to his father from 1915, in describing his love for autumn evenings, Lewis wrote,

> I love the afternoons now, don't you? There is something weird and desolate about the perfectly round orange coloured sun dropping down clear against a slatey grey sky seen through bare trees that pleases me better than all those cloud-cities and mountains that we used to see in summer . . . .[5]

Lewis only matured in his skill to sketch a vivid scene. In *Surprised by Joy*, Lewis mentioned that on his journey as a writer, he learned that writing meant suggesting, not stating, "I began . . . to look for expressions which would not merely state but suggest . . . I had learned what writing means."[6] The keen novelist *suggests*—that is, describes—rather than *states* or tells. The novelist creates a sensory world to be seen, heard, tasted, felt, and smelled.

Lewis knew how to work suggestion into his writing. When we come to the granular detail of his description, we get the feeling that we're being shown something more than mountains and trees:

---

3. Lewis, *Collected Letters* 2.864.

4. Lewis, *Boxen*, 149.

5. Lewis, *Collected Letters* 1.155.

6. Lewis, *Surprised by Joy*, 74.

> I stood at that moment with my back to the East and the mountains, and he, facing me, looked towards them. His face flushed with a new light. A fern, thirty yards behind him, turned golden. The eastern side of every tree-trunk grew bright. Shadows deepened. All the time there had been bird noises, trillings, chatterings, and the like; but now suddenly the full chorus was poured from every branch . . . .[7]

Yet any deeper meaning—whatever spiritual weight lies in this "new light"—must work through the subtleties of the description. It's writing like this that Coghill had in mind when he said of Lewis's prose works, "almost any page of almost any of them will yield sentences that a critical writer may envy."[8]

Young Lancaster had no greater example of the dictum, "describe it," than that which Lewis's works provided. The principle was core to Lewis's writing. He didn't add descriptive scenes to his plots. Rather, he created plots through description. No example serves better than what is arguably his best work of literature, *Till We Have Faces*. Throughout the novel, we feel the narrator Orual's internal struggle through the described external world:

> The struggle ended when we topped the last rise before the real Mountain. We were so high now that, though the sun was very strong, the wind blew bitterly cold. At our feet, between us and the Mountain, lay a cursed black valley: dark moss, dark peat-bogs, shingle, great boulders, and screes of stone sprawling down into it from the Mountain—as if the Mountain had sores and there were the stony issue from them. The great mass of it rose up (we tilted our heads back to look at it) into huge knobbles of stone against the sky, like an old giant's back teeth. The face it showed us was really no steeper than a roof, except for certain frightful cliffs on our left, but it looked as if it went up like a wall. It, too, was now black. Here the gods ceased trying to make me glad. There was nothing here that even the merriest heart could dance for.[9]

Moments of vivid sensory writing like this mark each of Lewis's novels. Readers enter into a world of sight, sound, and touch.

7. Lewis, *The Great Divorce*, 145.
8. Coghill, "The Approach to English," 65.
9. Lewis, *Till We Have Faces*, 97–98.

> Now he had come to a part of the wood where great globes of yellow fruit hung from the trees—clustered as toy-balloons are clustered on the back of the balloon-man and about the same size. He picked one of them and turned it over and over. The rind was smooth and firm and seemed impossible to tear open.[10]

Acclaimed English journalist and poet Stella Gibbons captured the way Lewis's writing shapes his reader's experience:

> His command of language astonishing, extraordinary, preternatural—for what can be more astonishing than to imagine the soil and scents and noises on a speck of fire millions of miles from the Earth so vividly that the reader can actually feel a nostalgia for them, as if they had been personally experienced?[11]

We have in Lewis an author whose imagination worked in subject and style. Thanks to talking beavers and buses to heaven, we're quick to recognize the former. But it's the latter, in its pictorial, definitive description that grants us moments of escape.

> A streak of dreary and disastrous dawn spread along the horizon, and widened and grew brighter, till in the end they hardly noticed the light of the stars who stood behind them. At last the sun came up.[12]

For the writer

Good writing doesn't tell; it shows. Just as no one in life goes about sharing every thought and feeling, so no good writer opens her characters up to the reader with explicitly confessional narration. Evocative, descriptive, sensory language allows the writer to create a vivid world. Descriptive language enables the writer to capture and convey the subtleties of the human condition. Lewis's adept ability to write descriptively serves as a model for which writers can strive.

Can you think of good descriptive writing examples? List them and explain what makes them good?

10. Lewis, *Perelandra*, 42.
11. Gibbons, "Imaginative Writing," 89.
12. Lewis, *The Last Battle*, 179.

Do try: To practice your descriptive writing, choose one of these two topics: the most beautiful place you've ever seen, or the most spiritually profound moment you've ever experienced. Now, write at least 750 words on your place or experience. Write this piece by going into great sensory detail and focusing on *showing*, rather than telling. Be vivid, auditory, tactile, and granular.

50

Words Too Big for the Subject

The final point of advice on good writing that Lewis gave Lancaster was:

> Don't use words too big for the subject. Don't say "infinitely" when
> you mean "very"; otherwise you'll have no word left when you
> want to talk about something really infinite.[1]

Lewis—equipped with an immense vocabulary and able to work in inimitable syntax—believed that good writing was characterized by tailored, controlled language. Not all subjects require big words, and even those that seemingly do would benefit from a simple, yet salient, substitution. This fifth rule has to do with proportion, the semantic balance between a word and the subject that word is meant to elucidate.

Lewis practiced proportional word choice. His writing emanates a self-imposed lexical limitation. He wrote with restraint, almost always choosing the straightforward necessary word instead of the over-exaggerated. If the value of a word is great (e.g., "infinitely") but the subject requires only a "very," then the writer should go with "very." Obviously, the writer will occasionally come across a scene or subject in need of large words—Lewis's explanation of spiritual awe required his using the word "Numinous"—but even in the most advanced instances, the goal is always the effectual essay, the poignant poem, the vivid novel.[2]

---

1. Hooper, *Collected Letters* 3.766.
2. Lewis, *The Problem of Pain*, 5.

Demonstrating how well Lewis chose words to suit his subjects is an embarrassment of riches. His every work effuses examples of the right use of the right word. One of my favorite examples of "don't use words too big for the subject" is *The Screwtape Letters*. Lewis's 1942 theological fantasy is more than a creative experiment in the diabolical discourse of virtue, vice, and the human condition—though it's not less. It's also an example of ordinary, conversational—but always precise—prose.

> Your man has been accustomed, ever since he was a boy, to have a dozen incompatible philosophies dancing about together inside his head.[3]

> The humans live in time but our Enemy destines them to eternity. He therefore, I believe, wants them to attend chiefly to two things, to eternity itself, and to that point of time which they call the Present. For the Present is the point at which time touches eternity.[4]

Screwtape may be a devil of hell, but he is an articulate one. And while we damn him for what says, we must give him credit for how he says it. As a model of good writing, of lucid sentences and tapered diction, *Screwtape* remains one of Lewis's finest works. The subject matter is eternally important, but Lewis's word choice remains tied to the temporal.

> He saw not only Them; he saw Him. This animal, this thing begotten in a bed, could look on Him. What is blinding, suffocating fire to you, is now cool light to him, is clarity itself, and wears the form of a Man.[5]

> All the delights of sense, or heart, or intellect, with which you could once have tempted him, even the delights of virtue itself, now seem to him in comparison but as the half nauseous attractions of a raddled harlot would seem to a man who hears that his true beloved whom he has loved all his life and whom he had believed to be dead is alive and even now at his door.[6]

---

3. Lewis, *The Screwtape Letters*, 4.
4. Ibid., 87.
5. Ibid., 186–87.
6. Ibid.

If overwriting is a sin, Lewis is absolved. While exaggerated language seems to be inherent in the mere act of writing, the writer's task is to exercise dominion over his diction. The writer has to choose the measured word to match the subject, reserving the big words for those subjects big enough to hold them. So when an idea called for a simple word, Lewis used a simple word. When what he wanted to say called for complex, weightier words, he employed appropriate language. There was a value system in Lewis's prose. Big subjects were worth big words, and small subjects deserved small words.

When writing about the challenge of modern education, Lewis used parataxis, simple linear, modifier-free syntax: "The task of the modern educator is not to cut down jungles but to irrigate deserts."[7]

Even when discussing what qualifies the ruling class to be the ruling class, Lewis spares the reader needlessly inflated words. Yet his message is clear:

> Culture is a bad qualification for a ruling class because it does not qualify men to rule. The things we really need in our rulers— mercy, financial integrity, practical intelligence, hard work, and the like—are no more likely to be found in cultured persons than in anyone else.[8]

Even in a theological poem on God's mercy and justice, Lewis writes in tapered language, constraining complicated themes to simple words in modest rhyme and meter:

> "Divine Justice"
> God in His mercy made
> The fixed pains of Hell.
> That misery might be stayed,
> God in His mercy made
> Eternal bounds and bade
> Its waves no further swell.
> God in His mercy made
> The fixed pains of Hell.[9]

One might ask when Lewis actually measured a subject and found it worth a big word, a word worth an "infinitely" and not a "very." The fact

---

7. Lewis, "Men without Chests," 14.

8. Lewis, "Lilies that Fester," 117.

9. Lewis, "Divine Justice," 98.

is that even when Lewis tackled complex subjects, his language remained conservative. This is yet another sign of Lewis's clarity. Works like "De Descriptione Temporum" or *The Four Loves* present a Lewis able to charge a sentence with strategically placed adjectives, or able to delve into a hypotactic sentence built on adverbs—but only when the subject called for it.

> The christening of Europe seemed to all our ancestors, whether they welcomed it themselves as Christians, or, like, Gibbon, deplored it as humanistic unbelievers, a unique, irreversible event.[10]

> The especial glory of Affection is that it can unite those who most emphatically, even comically, are not; people who, if they had not found themselves put down by fate in the same household or community, would have had nothing to do with each other.[11]

For the writer

Subject determines diction. And unless the subject requires an astronomically grandiose word, the writer should just use a very simple word. As a rule, only the large subjects require large words, and even the large words used for those large subjects should be clear, necessary for communicating the writer's ideas, and sparsely used. Most subjects do not require over-inflated diction—only those words painstakingly efficient, exact, and elucidating. And in all things: complex thought, simple language.

What direction does your diction usually take? The adjectivized and adverbially over-stated? Jargon? The intentionally erudite and academically impressive? How have you weighed a word's worth—by its rarity, complexity, its effectiveness in communicating an idea?

Do try: Take a potentially complex subject—the substance and function of the imagination, for example—and write a 500-word reflection using only accessible, understandable, and definite diction. Spend a few minutes reviewing why you went with the words you did and how you can revise for proportion to the subject and precision in communication.

10. Lewis, "De Descriptione Temporum," 13.

11. Lewis, *The Four Loves*, 36.

Conclusion
Do Try!

In the introduction I said that Lewis's writing style has influenced me more than that of any other prose writer, living or dead. But that doesn't quite capture it. It's his writing *life* that has influenced me more than any other writer. When I first set out on this book, I planned to write an academic work—a systematic treatment of the correlation and development of Lewis's epistolary advice on writing and its stylistic expressions across different fictive and non-fictive discourses. But that book wouldn't write.

As I read Lewis's letters and scoured back through his books, I came across moments when Lewis wrote to someone about how powerful the book he last read was. I learned how excited he was to keep working on a poem. I read his encouragement to another ambitious writer. It didn't take long before I stopped reading his advice on writing as material for a specialized book. I began to hear Lewis's words as if they were written to me. I started to take for myself Lewis's advice to Greeves, or Pitter, or Joan Lancaster. As I wrote, I shifted my book's audience from a niche group of Inkling specialists to anyone interested in Lewis, the craft of writing, or any combination of the two. What I thought would be a fascinating academic topic turned into a labor of love for Lewis and the innumerably powerful lessons he has to offer writers.

My hope is now only that writers who want to get better at their craft and who look up to Lewis as I do hear his voice through my simple presentation. I have tried to get out of the way as much as possible—hence the amount of primary source material, block quotes, and minimal analysis. There isn't anything I could hope to say that Lewis hasn't already said more clearly and convincingly. *C. S. Lewis and the Art of Writing* is meant to be an encouraging resource for writers, but I take a lion's share of encouragement for myself. Lewis's writing life has given me more personal perspective, more anecdotal wisdom, and more creative energy than any other author I've studied. There is something to learn in every chapter of his life in letters. I want to imitate his ravenous reading life, the way he allowed books to carve contours in his intellect and imagination. He convicts me to read more, and more deeply. Lewis admonishes me to read more receptively. To read good books over and over again.

As a writer, I'm challenged by Lewis's tenacious commitment to the craft. A love for writing remained the bedrock of his life. He kept writing through discouragement, failures, and success. I envy how he formed friendships because of and through writing. I want to seek out those relationships. I can relate to Lewis's habit of starting but not finishing books, his often self-critical stance toward his own work. Yet his prolific persistence in writing excellent literature gives hope to writers whose writing processes are often solid realities. Even in his frustrations and false starts, Lewis's creative life offers guidance to aspiring and experienced writers alike.

We have seen the makings of Lewis the writer, the essential role reading played in swaying his creativity, in seizing his every affection from an unimaginative life, and in shaping his most personal relationships. We've also surveyed some creative moments from his life in letters. We see, from the prosaic pages of "Animal Land" to *An Experiment on Criticism*, a writing life measured in line, page, and process. The priority Lewis gave to writing helps me understand how important it really is. Lewis wrote relentlessly. I want to, too. I want to follow the advice Lewis gave to Greeves: to "practice, practice, practice."

I have here tried to show Lewis to be a writer's writer, a wordsmith and literary craftsman from whom other writers may learn. His remarkable life in letters—with its attic beginnings reading Beatrice Potter and writing stories of Animal Land—serves as an exemplary model of devotion to the craft of writing. He generously gave guidance on prose and poetry to unknown and notable writers. We've seen how Lewis's advice to a young fan named Joan Lancaster provides a practical template for clear, plain, and exact prose.

In his essay, *The Weight of Glory*, Lewis said,

> There are no ordinary people. You have never talked to a mere mortal. Nations, cultures, arts, civilizations—these are mortal, and their life is to ours as the life of a gnat. But it is immortals whom

we joke with, work with, marry, snub, and exploit—immortal horrors or everlasting splendors.[1]

Lewis's high view of humanity holds true for writers. You've never met a mere writer. The ideas you have, those wild things your imagination conjures, and every word you write all spring from a mind made for immortality. You'll never write a mere word. Writing isn't an ephemeral endeavor. It's an essential one taken up by those made for eternity. That's why Lewis was so encouraging of it with others. It's on that point that I'll end, with the same admonishment to write that Lewis gave to others. In a letter written in the year before his death, Lewis encouraged a child named Jonathan to take up writing his own stories:

> Why don't you try writing some Narnian tales? I began to write when I was about your age, and it was the greatest fun. Do try![2]

And to another child, named Sydney, Lewis exhorted,

> I'm afraid I've said all I had to say about Narnia, and there will be no more of these stories. But why don't you try to write one yourself? I was writing stories before I was your age, and if you try, I'm sure you would find it great fun. Do![3]

C. S. Lewis and the Art of Writing isn't meant to be academically inaccessible. Nor is it meant to be purely informational. Those kinds of books would do you little good when you sat down to write. To be a better writer, you must first write something. Anything. Just write. And so to the writer, I say with Lewis, Do try!

1. Lewis, *The Weight of Glory*, 46.

2. Lewis, *Letters to Children*, 99.

3. Ibid., 101–2. In that same year, Lewis, weakened by failing a prostate, kidneys, and heart, and uninterested in returning to the Narnia narratives, answered a Denise admonishing her to continue the stories. Lewis wrote, "I am delighted to hear that you liked the Narnian books, and it was nice of you to write and tell me. There *is* a map at the end of some of them in some editions. But why not do one yourself! And why not write stories for yourself to fill up the gaps in Narnian history? I've left you plenty of hints—especially where Lucy and the Unicorn are talking in *The Last Battle*. I feel *I* have done all I can!" Ibid., 104.

Bibliography

Adey, Lionel. *C. S. Lewis: Writer, Dreamer, and Mentor.* Grand Rapids: Eerdmans, 1998.

Bailey, George. "In the University." In *C. S. Lewis: Speaker & Teacher,* edited by Carolyn Keefe, 79–94. Grand Rapids: Zondervan, 1971.

Barfield, Owen. *On C. S. Lewis.* Oxford: Barfield, 2011.

Bennett, J. A. W. "'Grete Clerk.'" In *Light on C. S. Lewis,* edited by Jocelyn Gibb, 44–50. London: Bles, 1965.

Boehme, Jacob. *The Signature of All Things.* London: Dent, 1912.

Calhoun, Scott. "C. S. Lewis as Philologist: Studies in Words." In *C. S. Lewis: Life, Works, and Legacy,* edited by Bruce Edwards, 4:81–98. Westport, CT: Praeger. 2007.

Carpenter, Humphrey. *The Inklings.* London: Allen & Unwin, 1978.

Coghill, Nelvill. "The Approach to English." In *Light on C. S. Lewis,* edited by Jocelyn Gibb, 51–66. London: Bles, 1965.

Como, James, ed. *Remembering C. S. Lewis.* San Francisco: Ignatius, 1979.

Coleridge, Samuel Taylor. *Biographia Literaria.* London: Oxford University Press, 1985.

Dorsett, Lyle. *Seeking the Secret Place: The Spiritual Formation of C. S. Lewis.* Grand Rapids: Brazos, 2004.

Downing, David. *The Most Reluctant Convert.* Downers Grove, IL: IVP, 2002.

Dunckel, Mona. "C. S. Lewis as Allegorist." In *C. S. Lewis: Life, Works, and Legacy,* edited by Bruce Edwards, 3:29–49. Westport, CT: Praeger. 2007.

Duriez, Colin. *The C. S. Lewis Chronicles.* New York: BlueBridge, 2005.

Edwards, Bruce, ed. *C. S. Lewis: The Life, Works, and Legacy.* 4 vols. Westport, CT: Praeger, 2007.

Farrer, Austin. "The Christian Apologist." In *Light on C. S. Lewis,* edited by Jocelyn Gibb, 23–43. London: Bles, 1965.

Ford, Paul. *Yours, Jack: Spiritual Direction from C. S. Lewis.* New York: Harper One, 2008.

Gibb, Jocelyn, ed. *Light on C. S. Lewis.* London: Bles, 1965.

Gibbons, Stella. "Imaginative Writing." In *Light on C. S. Lewis,* edited by Jocelyn Gibb, 86–101. London: Bles, 1965.

Gibson, Evan K. *C. S. Lewis: Spinner of Tales: A Guide to His Fiction.* Washington, DC: Christian University Press, 1980.

Glyer, Diana Pavlac. *The Company They Keep: C. S. Lewis and J. R. R. Tolkien as Writers in Community.* Kent, OH: Ohio University Press, 2007.

Goffar, Janine. *C. S. Lewis Index: Rumours from the Sculptor's Shop.* Riverside, CA: La Sierra University Press, 1997.

Bibliography

Graham, David, ed. *We Remember C. S. Lewis: Essays & Memoirs.* Nashville: Broadman & Holman, 2001.

Green, Roger Lancelyn, and Walter Hooper. *C. S. Lewis: A Biography.* London: Collins, 1974.

Greene, Graham. *Collected Essays.* New York: Penguin, 1981.

Hooper, Walter, ed. *The Collected Letters of C. S. Lewis.* 3 vols. New York: HarperCollins, 2004–7.

———. *C. S. Lewis: Companion & Guide.* New York: HarperCollins, 1996.

———. "Introduction" to C. S. Lewis, *Boxen.* London: Harcourt, 1985.

———. "Introduction" to C. S. Lewis, *Present Concerns.* New York: Harcourt, 1986.

———, ed. *They Stand Together: The Letters of C. S. Lewis to Arthur Greeves (1914–1963).* New York: MacMillan, 1979.

Howard, Thomas. *C. S. Lewis: Man of Letters.* San Francisco: Ignatius, 1987.

Hutter, Charles, ed. *Imagination and the Spirit.* Grand Rapid: Eerdmans, 1971.

Jacobs, Alan. *The Narnian: The Life and Imagination of C. S. Lewis.* San Francisco: Harper, 2005.

James, Richard. "Lewis's Early Schooling." In *C. S. Lewis: Life, Works, and Legacy,* edited by Bruce Edwards, 1:45–78. Westport, CT: Praeger. 2007.

Keefe, Carolyn, ed. *C. S. Lewis: Speaker & Teacher.* Grand Rapids: Zondervan, 1971.

King, Don. *C. S. Lewis, Poet.* Kent, OH: Kent State University Press, 2001.

Lewis, C. S. *All My Road Before Me: The Diary of C. S. Lewis 1922–1927.* New York: Harcourt, 1991.

———. *Boxen: The Imaginary World of the Young C. S. Lewis.* Edited by Walter Hooper. London: Harcourt, 1985.

———. "Cross-Examination." In *God in the Dock,* edited by Walter Hooper, 258–70. Grand Rapids: Eerdmans, 1970.

———. *The Dark Tower and Other Stories.* New York: Harcourt, 1977.

———. "De Descriptione Temporum." In *They Asked for a Paper,* 9–25. London: Bles, 1962.

———. "Divine Justice." In *Poems,* 98. New York: Harcourt, 1964.

———. *Dymer.* 1926. Reprint. London: Dent 1950.

———. "The Efficacy of Prayer." In *The World's Last Night and Other Essays,* 3–13. New York: Harcourt, 1960.

———. *English Literature in the Sixteenth Century Excluding Drama.* The Oxford History of English Literature 3. Oxford: Clarendon, 1954.

———. "Equality." In *Present Concerns,* edited by Walter Hooper, 17–20, New York: Harcourt, 1986.

———, ed. *Essays Presented to Charles Williams.* Grand Rapids: Eerdmans, 1966.

———. *An Experiment in Criticism.* Cambridge: Cambridge University Press, 1961.

———. *The Four Loves.* New York: Harcourt, 1960.

———. ed. *George MacDonald: An Anthology.* San Francisco: HarperCollins, 2001.

———. *The Great Divorce.* New York: Harper Collins, 2001.

———. *A Grief Observed.* San Francisco: HarperCollins, 2001.

———. "Hamlet: The Prince or The Poem?" In *They Asked for a Paper,* 51–71. London: Bles, 1962.

———. *The Horse and His Boy.* New York: HarperCollins, 1994.

———. "Is English Doomed?" In *Present Concerns,* edited by Walter Hooper, 27–31. New York: Harcourt, 1986.

————. "It All Began with a Picture." In *On Stories*, 53–54. New York: Harcourt, 1982.

————. "The Language of Religion." In *The Seeing Eye*, edited by Walter Hooper, 171–88. New York: Ballantine, 1967.

————. *The Last Battle*. New York: HarperCollins, 1994.

————. *Letters to an American Lady*. Edited by Clyde Kilby. Grand Rapids: Eerdmans, 1967.

————. *Letters to Children*. Edited by Lyle W. Dorsett et al. New York: Touchstone, 1995.

————. *Letters to Malcolm*. New York: Harcourt, 1964.

————. "Lilies that Fester." In *They Asked for a Paper*, 105–19. London: Bles, 1962.

————. *The Lion, the Witch and the Wardrobe*. New York: HarperCollins, 1994.

————. *The Magician's Nephew*. New York: HarperCollins, 1994.

————. "Men without Chests." In *The Abolition of Man*, 1–26. New York: HarperCollins, 2001.

————. *Mere Christianity*. New York: HarperCollins, 2001.

————. "Myth Became Fact." In *God in the Dock*, edited by Walter Hooper, 63–68. Grand Rapids: Eerdmans, 1970.

————. "The Nameless Isle." In *Narrative Poems*, edited by Walter Hooper, 105–28. New York: Harcourt, 1979.

————. "On Stories." In *On Stories*, edited by Walter Hooper, 3–20. San Francisco: Harvest, 1982.

————. "On Three Ways of Writing Children." In *On Stories*, edited by Walter Hooper, 31–43. San Francisco: Harvest, 1982.

————. *Out of the Silent Planet*. New York: Macmillan, 1965.

————. *Perelandra*. New York: Macmillan, 1965.

————. *The Pilgrim's Regress*. Wade Annotated Edition. Grand Rapids: Eerdmans, 2014.

————. *Prince Caspian*. New York: HarperCollins, 1994.

————. *The Problem of Pain*. New York: HarperCollins, 2000.

————. *Poems*. New York: Harcourt, 1964.

————. *Reflections on the Psalms*. 1958. Reprint. New York: Harcourt, 1986.

————. *The Screwtape Letters*. Annotated Edition. New York: HarperOne, 2013.

————. *The Silver Chair*. New York: HarperCollins, 1994.

————. "Sometimes Fairy Stories May Say Best What's to be Said." In *On Stories*, edited by Walter Hooper, 45–48. San Francisco: Harvest, 1982.

————. *Spirits in Bondage*. New York: Harcourt, 1984.

————. *Studies in Words*. Cambridge: Cambridge University Press, 1990.

————. *Surprised by Joy*. New York: Harcourt, 1955.

————. *That Hideous Strength*. New York: Macmillan, 1965.

————. *They Asked for a Paper: Papers and Addresses*. London: Bles, 1962.

————. *Till We Have Faces*. New York: Harcourt, 1984.

————. *The Voyage of the Dawn Treader*. New York: HarperCollins, 1994.

————. *The Weight of Glory*. New York: Harcourt, 2000.

Lewis, Warren. *Brothers and Friends: The Diaries of Major Warren Hamilton Lewis*. San Francisco: Harper & Row, 1982.

————, ed. *The Lewis Papers*. 11 vols. 1933–1935. Located at The Marion E. Wade Center, Wheaton College, IL.

Manlove, Colin. *The Chronicles of Narnia: The Patterning of a Fantastic World*. New York: Twayne, 1993.

MacDonald, George. "The Imagination: Its Functions and Its Culture." In *A Dish of Orts*, 1–28. London: Sampson Low Marston, 1893.

———. *Lilith*. London: Chatto & Windus, 1895.

McGrath, Alister. *The Intellectual World of C. S. Lewis*. Oxford: Wiley-Blackwell, 2014.

Raine, "From a Poet." In *Light on C. S. Lewis*, edited by Jocelyn Gibb, 102–5. London: Bles, 1965.

Rogers, Mary. "Rejected by Oxford." *Oxford Today: The University Magazine*, Michaelmas, 1998, 53–55.

Ryken, Leland. *Windows to the World: Literature in Christian Perspective*. Eugene, OR: Wipf & Stock, 2000.

Sayer, George. *Jack*. Wheaton, IL: Crossway, 1994.

Schakel, Peter, and Charles Huttar, eds. *Imagination and the Arts in C. S. Lewis: Journeying to Narnia and Other Worlds*. Columbia: University of Missouri Press, 2002.

Taylor, Jeremy. *Whole Works*. 5 vols. Edited by R. Heber. London, 1822.

Terentianus. *De syllabis*. Edited and translated by J. W. Beck. Göttingen: Vandenhoeck & Ruprecht, 1992.

Tibullus. *Tibullus: A Commentary*. Norman, OK: University of Oklahoma Press, 1973.

Tolkien, J. R. R. "On Faerie-Stories." In *The Monster and the Critics*, edited by Christopher Tolkien, 109–61. New York: HarperCollins, 2006.

———. *The Letters of J. R. R. Tolkien*. Edited by Humphrey Carpenter. New York: Houghton Mifflin, 2000.

Werther, David, and Susan Werther, eds. *C. S. Lewis's List: The Ten Books that Influenced Him Most*. New York: Bloomsbury, 2015.

Wirt, Sherwood. "Heaven, Earth, and Outer Space." *Decision* II, 1963, 4.

Zaleski, Philip, and Carol Zaleski. *The Fellowship: The Literary Lives of the Inklings*. New York: Farrar, Straus and Giroux, 2015.

Index

Index

p 69 Intimacy w/ reading

p74 on time/the idea that all moments
    are present to God

p110 the writer births his idea/whether
    it leads a full life or/not no
    matter

p119 new generations rise up and
    destroy the achievements of the
    previous generations

p170 (see 169 'inspired' by this Cy)
    "... diabolically convincing discourse in"

p178 ... impulse ... (read fairy tale)
    imaginative incubation
    find form ... (fable (short story))
        (novel)
    — staying attuned to insistent
    mental images
        (Mrs. Goye Thomas)

Printed in Great Britain
by Amazon

46079004R00142